D0811892

Barb & Bill
Christmas 1999
Happy New Mill
Jodi Gay &
"the girls"

ULTIMATE
CHRISTMAS

ULTIMATE
CHRISTMAS

JANE NEWDICK

The Reader's Digest Association

(Canada) Ltd.

MONTREAL

A Dorling Kindersley Book

Project Editor Annabel Martin
Art Editors Kate Scott, Kylie Mulquin
Senior Art Editor Tracey Clarke
Food Editor Alexa Stace

Photography Dave King
Food Photography Martin Brigdale
Recipes Janice Murfitt

Managing Editor Susannah Marriott
Managing Art Editor Toni Kay

D.T.P. Designer Karen Ruane
Production Controller Patricia Harrington

Published in Canada in 1996 by
The Reader's Digest Association (Canada) Ltd.
215 Redfern Avenue, Westmount, Quebec H3Z 2V9

First published in Great Britain in 1996 by
Dorling Kindersley Limited,
9 Henrietta Street, London WC2E 8PS

Copyright © 1996 Dorling Kindersley Limited, London
Text copyright © 1996 Jane Newdick

All rights reserved. No part of this publication may be
reproduced, stored in a retrieval system, or transmitted in
any form or by any means, electronic, mechanical,
photocopying, recording or otherwise, without the prior
written permission of the copyright owner.

CANADIAN CATALOGUING IN PUBLICATION DATA

Newdick, Jane
    Ultimate Christmas

Includes index.
ISBN 0-88850-540-X

    1. Christmas decorations.   2. Christmas cookery.
3. Christmas   I. Title

GT4985.N49 1996   394.2'663   C96-900291-2

READER'S DIGEST and the Pegasus logo are registered
trademarks of The Reader's Digest Association, Inc.

Reproduced by Colourscan, Singapore
Printed and bound in Great Britain
by Butler & Tanner Ltd.

96 97 98 99 / 5 4 3 2 1

CONTENTS

INTRODUCTION 6
A HISTORY OF CHRISTMAS 8

A GALLERY OF CHRISTMAS TREES 12

WREATHS, GARLANDS, & FLOWERS 48

INTRODUCTION

THESE DAYS IT WOULD BE VERY EASY to get everything you need for a perfect Christmas in one expensive and exhausting shopping spree. For two or three months each year, stores try to tempt us with a bewildering choice of Christmas items: food from around the world, sophisticated decorations, glamorous gifts, even ready-decorated trees complete with lights. It seems we have come a long way from the days of decorating the house with a branch of evergreen and slipping a tangerine and a wooden toy into a child's stocking, but along this route to such plenty we are at risk of losing the very pleasures and delights of getting involved in the real preparations for festivity. The satisfaction of making and giving gifts, cooking family recipes, carefully unpacking heirloom decorations, or weaving a simple door wreath is immeasurable, and it all builds up toward the excitement of the day itself. In a rush to have everything bigger, newer, or better we lose out by ignoring our own creativity and forgetting that a gift, homemade and carefully wrapped, will charm the recipient a hundred times more than an impersonal store-bought present.

Homemade, however, does not have to mean quaint and unsophisticated – today we have such a superb choice of ingredients and materials that making things for Christmas has never been easier. There are luxurious papers, glossy paints, vivid fabrics, ornate beads, gold leaf, gilding cremes, fresh and preserved fruit, leaves and flowers, thin, fat, short, and tall candles in all sorts of colors, intricate ribbons, and much, much more.

Another important part of Christmas is the food we eat to celebrate with friends and family. The availability of ingredients from around the world makes Christmas an excellent time to experiment with recipes from other cultures in addition to cooking the well-loved dishes from our own countries that do so much to give us a sense of continuity and security in our often hectic lives.

While many of us do not have the confidence to make everyday things ourselves, presuming bought to be best, there does seem to be more of a tradition for having a go with Christmas decorations, whether a table centerpiece with candles and flowers, greetings cards decorated with a stamped motif, or just a personalized gift wrapping. The secret is to begin by attempting things that come easily to you: if you can sew, try making some luxurious fabric tree decorations; while if the most you can handle is a tube of glue, stick seeds on a foam ball to make beautiful natural baubles. The cooks among us would probably prefer to create a bunch of cookie shapes to thread as tree decorations, but even the most untalented creators can string fruit and popcorn into garlands to wind through the tree's branches.

Small successes help you gain the confidence to experiment more, and to enjoy the process of making and doing, discovering a great pleasure in working at your own speed surrounded by exquisite ingredients. If you have invested your precious time, love, and creativity into the projects, they cannot fail to be fabulous. Good luck in making one or all of the ideas in the book – may this Christmas be the first "ultimate Christmas" of many.

Jane Newdick

THE HISTORY OF CHRISTMAS

A CHILD DISCOVERING the delights of Christmas for the first time
is presented with a wonderful array of good things: trees with
sparkling lights, carol singers, rich food such as iced cakes and
cookies, presents tucked into bulging stockings, and
days of excitement and parties. The modern
Christmas is in fact a cornucopia of widely
different traditions. Some traditions come
from religious sources or social customs; others
originated in folklore and magic. Over time,
the secular and religious traditions have become
entwined and embellished in a fascinating ritual.

Deck the Halls
*Victorian Christmas
cards show homes
adorned with
evergreen boughs*

CHRISTMAS DAY
Feasts held in deep midwinter to celebrate the winter
solstice, or shortest day, were common long before Christianity,
and have been traced across Europe to ancient Babylon and Egypt.
One of the most notable was the Roman Saturnalia, from December
17 to 24. The Christian church chose various dates for Christ's
birthday before settling finally on December 25, a deliberate
substitution for the pagan festival celebrating the rebirth of light in
the winter gloom. Some of the rituals and customs used in the pagan
celebrations, such as the "greening" of public buildings and houses
with branches, were also rapidly absorbed by the Christian church.

THE TREE AND EVERGREENS
Tree worship dates back to prehistoric times, and the Christmas tree
probably has pagan origins, being an evergreen and thus the one tree
in the forest with the promise of survival until spring. Fir trees
decorated with apples, paper flowers, and candles were introduced
into Pennsylvania in the early 19th century by German immigrants,
and became popular throughout the US by midcentury. President
Franklin Pierce put the first Christmas tree in the White House
in 1856. In Britain, Prince Albert, the German-born husband of

Queen Victoria, had popularized Christmas trees, and introduced decorations made from spun glass, miniature wooden toys, and paper ornaments. A picture of the royal tree, minus the royal symbols, appeared in a US magazine in 1850, stimulating North Americans to make decorated trees part of their own traditions. By the end of the 19th century, decorations were being made commercially, and now most people buy mass-produced baubles, tinsel, and other decorations rather than making their own.

Green boughs, mistletoe, and holly were all used in pagan celebrations long before the advent of Christianity. The Celtic Druids believed that mistletoe warded off evil and promoted fertility. Other cultures used it too, including the Greeks and Romans, and in Norse mythology it represented peace. While holly was adopted by the Christian church – its red berries symbolizing Christ's blood – mistletoe with its powerful pagan symbolism was banned in churches, though no doorway is complete without a bunch of mistletoe or a kissing bough.

Craft Dough Crowns
(See pages 20–21)
Decorate a traditional tree with homemade craft dough shapes

CARDS AND GIFTS

The ancient Romans gave lavish gifts to each other during the feast days of the Saturnalia, but it took many more centuries to see a widespread adoption of this present-giving. Not until the late 19th century and the beginnings of consumerism did it become usual to give and receive gifts. Originally, these simple homemade offerings were not wrapped, but they later came to be elaborately presented in special boxes and papers to signify the season.

Cards were yet another Victorian addition to Christmas. At first they were quite unseasonal in their designs, occasionally bawdy and usually sentimental. Images such as the robin and snow scenes became popular with the advent of color printing. In 1843 Henry Cole, a founder of the Victoria and Albert Museum in London, commissioned the first card.

Traditional Christmas Card
The sending of Christmas cards dates back to the mid-19th century

The early 1850s saw the first American-made Christmas card. It was a combination of season's greetings and self-promotion by the card's distributor, R.H. Pease, who operated a variety store in Albany, New York.

THE ORIGIN OF SANTA

Santa Claus, Father Christmas, St. Nicholas, and Sinterklaas are basically all the same person, descended from the Roman King of the Saturnalia. The original St. Nicholas was a fourth-century saint. His cult became popular in the Middle Ages, and in Switzerland, Germany, and the Netherlands he was linked with gift-giving on his feast day, December 6. The reindeer probably came from stories of the Norse god Woden who rode through the sky with reindeer and 42 ghostly huntsmen. Clement Moore's famous poem *A Visit from St. Nicholas* ("Twas the night before Christmas") sealed the image of Santa Claus, his reindeer, and the magical flying sleigh loaded with sacks of presents. The image of a white-bearded man in a red and white suit is very recent. A century ago, Santa Claus was usually depicted in a long brown robe or furs carrying a cross and wine flask with a holly crown on his head. In 1885 a Boston printer, Louis Prang, first devised the red-suited Santa and this theme was later developed by the Coca Cola advertising artist Haddon Sundblom in the 1930s, producing the modern image of a jolly character in a red suit trimmed with white fur.

Santa Claus
Santa started out in brown robes, but is recognized today by his red suit and white beard

CUSTOMS AND TRADITIONS

There arc endless games and pastimes, quaint customs, and odd traditions that happen only at this time of year. Many, such as the yule log, originated far in the past. To most people this is now a delicious log-shaped chocolate cake, but originally the yule log was dragged home from the woods with much ceremony and lit on Christmas

Eve to symbolize the sun and its warmth. An Englishman named Tom Smith invented the tube-shaped cracker, with a fire cracker inside to produce the bang. The paper hat in the cracker may be related to the hats worn in Tudor times by the Lords of Misrule, who were the leaders of the Christmas revels. Games, singing, and dancing were all seasonal entertainments and still are, albeit in very different forms. The singing of Christmas carols in the streets, a tradition imported into the US from England, began in Boston during the 1890s and soon spread throughout the country. Centuries ago in Europe, people gathered on the dark nights of the winter solstice and broke into merriment and wild behavior, fueled by ample food and drink. Not much changes! Pantomimes in England have a long tradition, and usually include role reversal of the sexes and of authority, and dressing up. The modern version can be traced through Saturnalian festivities and mumming plays to the 18th-century harlequinades.

Tree Baubles
Colored glass baubles are designed to catch the light

FOOD AND FEASTS

The concentration on food and feasting at Christmas is not surprising – before the days of canning and freezing, it was hard to survive the winter without stores of preserved food. Summer preserves and the last of the fresh food were brought out, while hardship was forgotten for a brief time of merrymaking. Some traditional recipes hark back to times when foods such as dried fruit and nuts were luxuries saved for feasting. Spices and flavorings are important in many recipes, echoing earlier dishes in which these precious ingredients were gathered from all over the known world. Most countries have dishes that are special to this time, such as the heavy fruit cake and round Christmas pudding from Britain, and the spiced cakes, cookies, and breads of central Europe.

Roast Turkey with Cornbread Stuffing
(See page 159 for recipe)
Serve with cranberries, blueberries, pumpkin, and roasted chestnuts

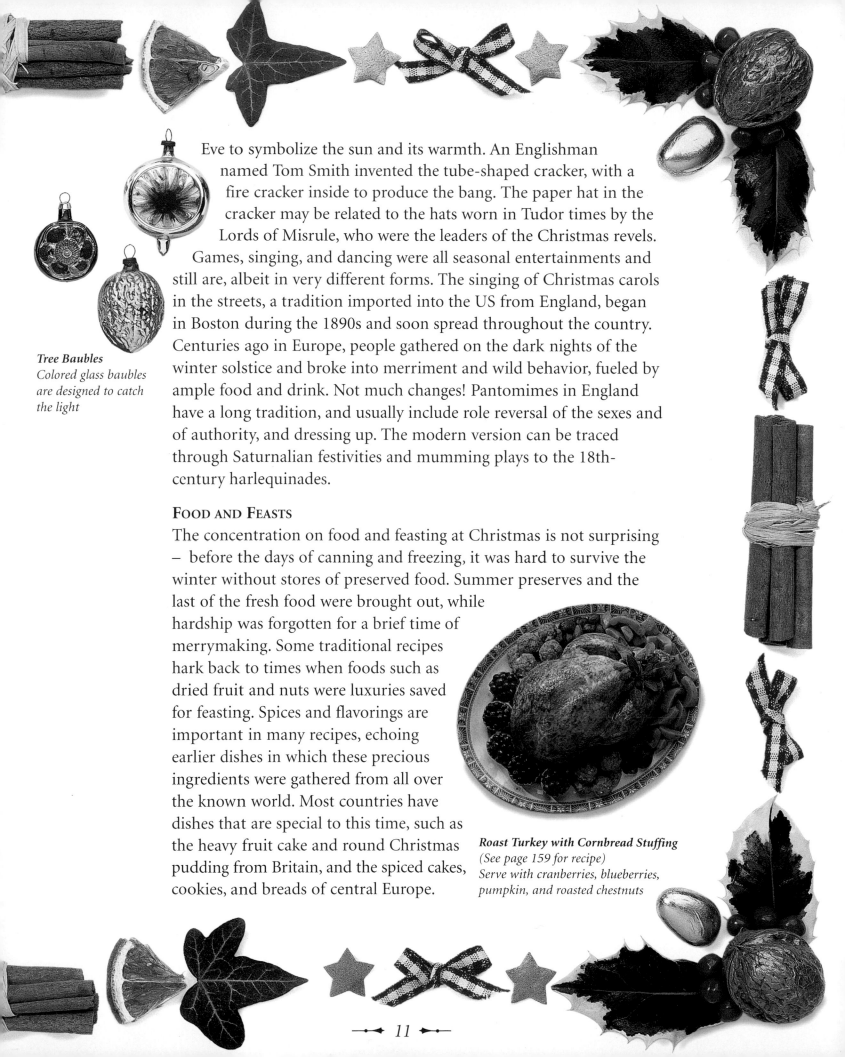

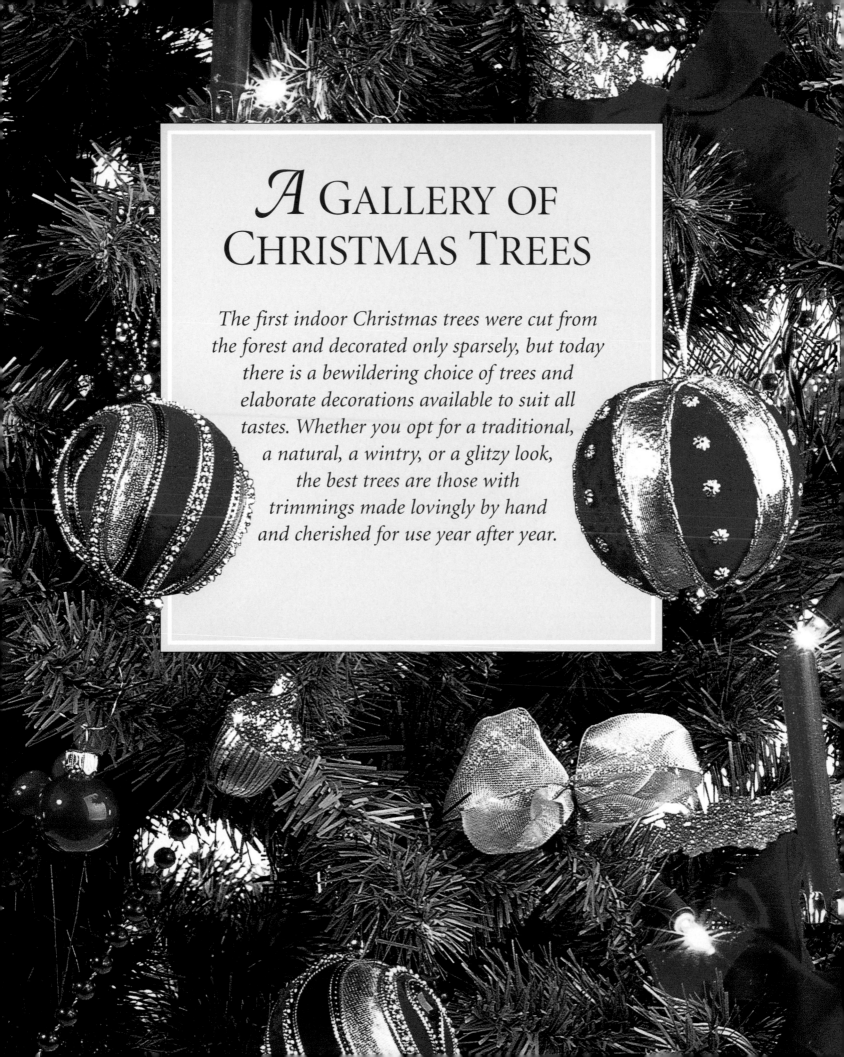

A GALLERY OF CHRISTMAS TREES

The first indoor Christmas trees were cut from the forest and decorated only sparsely, but today there is a bewildering choice of trees and elaborate decorations available to suit all tastes. Whether you opt for a traditional, a natural, a wintry, or a glitzy look, the best trees are those with trimmings made lovingly by hand and cherished for use year after year.

SELECTING TREES & CONTAINERS

WITH SO MANY CHRISTMAS TREES available, we can have whatever we want – will you enjoy the evocative scent of a cut or potted fresh tree, the convenience of an artificial tree, or something modern, stylish, and completely different? The answer depends on your purposes; it helps to consider cost, available space, and how long the tree needs to last. Once the tree is chosen, select a container to match.

BLUE SPRUCE
(See also page 19)
This prickly tree takes its name from its exceptional blue tinge, which looks fabulous with red and gold decorations. It retains its large needles quite well, but those that fall can be painful to step on.

REAL TREES

Choose a potted tree with roots if you wish to replant it after Christmas. Alternatively, a cut tree can retain its needles quite well if placed in water.

Small, glossy leaves

Characteristic spiky, blue-green needles

BAY TREE (See also page 44)
This small leafy tree with a neat round shape is unusual, but ideal for a small room. Keep it in a pot, water it regularly, and dress it with scaled-down decorations for Christmas. If you prefer, bays are available from garden centers, clipped in the classic pine tree shape.

Variegated leaves add color to the tree

HOLLY TREE (See also page 28)
Instead of using just a few sprigs of festive holly, why not bring the whole tree indoors for Christmas? Choose a holly tree in glossy green with red berries, a cultivar on a long stem, or an interesting variety with variegated leaves.

Pretty cane container hides a functional watertight pot

NORDMAN (See also page 29)
A soft and bushy fir tree that tends to retain its glossy green needles, making it ideal to cut and keep indoors. The layered branches are easy to decorate.

SCOTS PINE (See also page 33)
This popular tree should retain its needles throughout the Christmas period. Take care when hanging glass baubles on the ends of the soft branches; they can easily slip off.

Containers

Place rooted trees in watertight containers filled with damp soil, and put cut trees in water, soil, or sand.

Steel bucket, practical for a real tree, is easily filled with soil or water.

Decorated terracotta pot must be glazed if filled with damp soil.

Terracotta pot is ideal for all trees, and is inexpensive and easy to paint.

Copper bucket suits the colors of real trees rather than artificial ones.

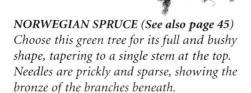

NORWEGIAN SPRUCE (See also page 45)
Choose this green tree for its full and bushy shape, tapering to a single stem at the top. Needles are prickly and sparse, showing the bronze of the branches beneath.

Decorated wicker container hides a watertight pot

ARTIFICIAL TREES

A high-quality artificial tree can be used for years.
If storage space is at a premium, opt for one that can
be dismantled. Styles are not limited to fir trees –
imaginative alternatives are available to suit all tastes.

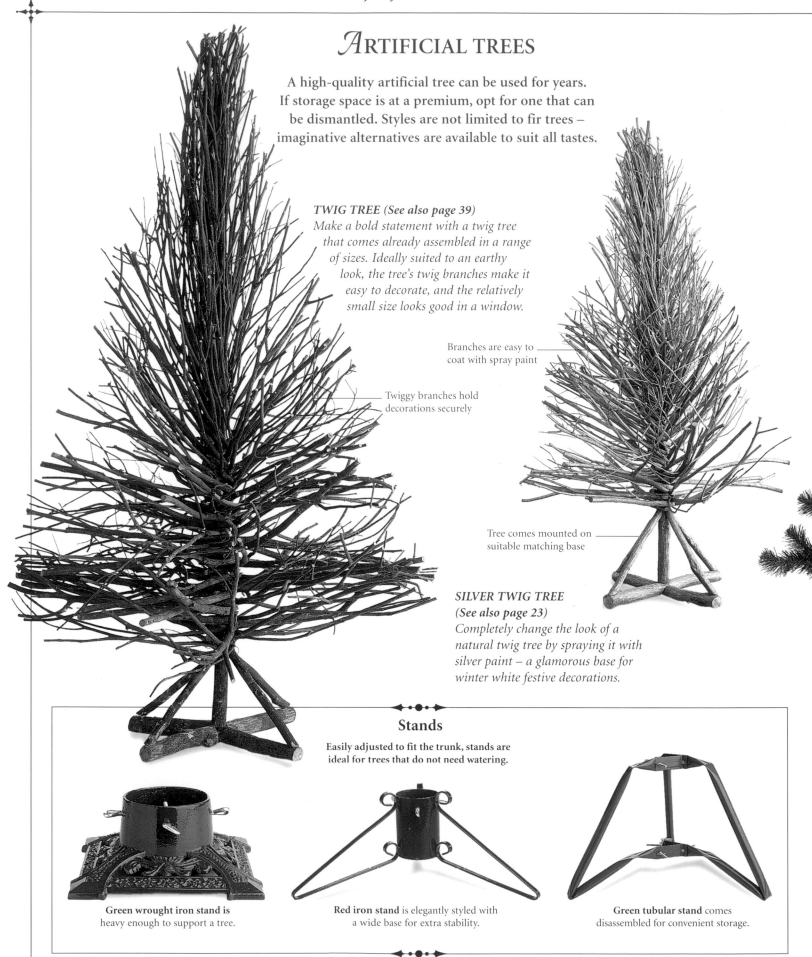

TWIG TREE *(See also page 39)*
*Make a bold statement with a twig tree
that comes already assembled in a range
of sizes. Ideally suited to an earthy
look, the tree's twig branches make it
easy to decorate, and the relatively
small size looks good in a window.*

Branches are easy to
coat with spray paint

Twiggy branches hold
decorations securely

Tree comes mounted on
suitable matching base

SILVER TWIG TREE
(See also page 23)
*Completely change the look of a
natural twig tree by spraying it with
silver paint – a glamorous base for
winter white festive decorations.*

Stands

**Easily adjusted to fit the trunk, stands are
ideal for trees that do not need watering.**

Green wrought iron stand is
heavy enough to support a tree.

Red iron stand is elegantly styled with
a wide base for extra stability.

Green tubular stand comes
disassembled for convenient storage.

Each branch hooks
into the trunk for
easy assembly

Branches can be
tweaked to produce
the desired shape

METAL TREE (See also page 32)
*An elegant metal tree is perfect for
a modern, minimalist look that
demands simple but well thought-out
decorations. Leave it in position all year
round and dress it up for Christmas.*

Curled branches are
ideal for hanging
decorations on

Shades of brown and
green make branches
look realistic

Pot made from strips
of pine encircled by
steel bands

ARTIFICIAL TREE
(See also pages 18, 22, 38)
*A convincing artificial fir tree can be bent
into a perfect shape and never drops its
needles. Invest in a good one and it will last
for years before beginning to look tired.*

Gold-colored metal
with a matte finish

Wide base stops
heavy tree from
toppling over

TRADITIONAL TREES

REGAL RED AND GOLD are used to give these classic trees a traditional festive look, mixing old-fashioned and handmade decorations with modern, store-bought baubles. Wired bows, cranberry rings, and craft dough shapes jostle for pride of place with glitzy gold tassels and garlands of ruby red beads, while wax candles add a timeless quality.

ANTIQUE LOOK
Smother an artificial tree with a thousand and one red and gold decorations, from heirlooms passed down the generations to new classic baubles with a twist. Lighting wax candles on the tree is not recommended, so use white Christmas lights for sparkle.

Cranberry ring shines among the baubles

Garland of red beads spirals down the tree

Begin by winding white Christmas lights around the tree

Glossy glass balls fill in gaps

Position large velvet baubles where they will catch the light

Add tiny baskets of candy on lower branches

Velvet cheat's bow (see page 105)

Red-painted terracotta pot adorned with large bow and tassel

WE THREE KINGS
Choose a traditional crimson and gold theme to complement a beautiful blue spruce tree, using golden camels, opulent eastern crowns, and sparkling strings of stars to tell the Christmas story. Finish with scarlet berries, thick shining tassels, gold snowflakes, and iridescent baubles.

Bunch of holly berries

Weave a garland of gold stars among the branches

Gilded craft dough camel (see page 20)

Jeweled crowns (see page 21)

Mirrored stars

Scatter oversized tassels randomly on the branches

Terracotta pot contains damp soil to keep tree fresh

MAKING THE CRAFT DOUGH CAMELS

One recipe of dough will make about ten camels, but if you need fewer, unbaked dough will last for several weeks wrapped in plastic wrap and kept in the refrigerator. Painting the shapes with a coat of varnish gives extra protection and shine.

◆ EQUIPMENT ◆

Pencil
Cardboard
Scissors
Cutting mat
Mixing bowl
Wooden spoon
Water
Flour, to dust
Rolling pin
Kitchen knife
Garlic press
Baking tray
Pin
Wire rack
Paintbrush
Varnish (optional)
Glue

Ingredients

Gold paint

Red paint

6in (15cm) cord

30 tiny beads

2 cups flour

1 cup salt

1 Using the template on page 187, draw a camel on a piece of cardboard and cut it out carefully with a craft knife.

2 Mix the flour and salt in a bowl, then gradually stir in 1 cup of water to make a dry but workable mixture.

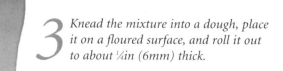

3 Knead the mixture into a dough, place it on a floured surface, and roll it out to about ¼in (6mm) thick.

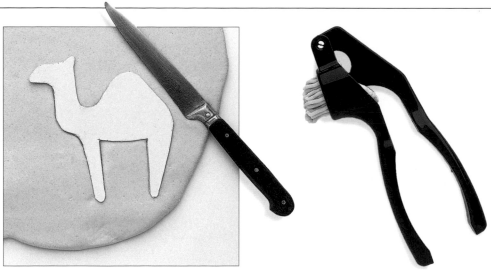

4 Place the template on the dough and cut around it with a sharp knife. Repeat to make a total of ten camels.

5 Cut and engrave a little piece of dough to make a saddle for each camel, and push more dough through a garlic press to make a fringe for the saddle. Position these details on the camels ready for baking.

6 Place the camels on a baking tray and bake on the lowest setting for about 4 hours, or until the dough is hard but not brown. Prick the back of the camel with a pin to test for firmness. Cool on a wire rack.

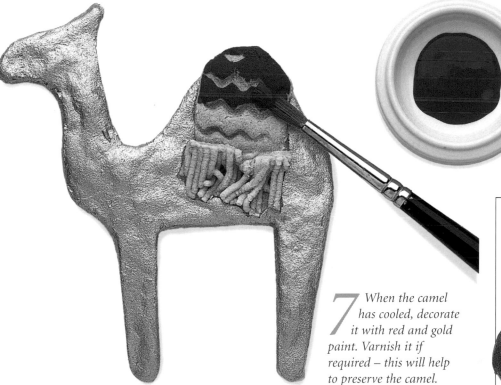

7 When the camel has cooled, decorate it with red and gold paint. Varnish it if required – this will help to preserve the camel.

8 Loop a piece of gold cord and glue it to the back for hanging. Glue tiny beads to the saddle to finish.

Jeweled Crowns

Use the same method to make craft dough crowns that hang from the tree on loops of gold cord. Add intricate details, paint them red and gold, and decorate with sparkly gold beads. Glue a loop of cord to the back to finish.

WHITE TREES

THESE GLITTERING TREES topped with silver stars sparkle like winter frost in the early morning sun. The delicate branches are laden with decorations made from frosted glass, translucent mother-of-pearl, masses of shimmering sequins, gleaming silver ribbon, and shells wrapped in decadent lengths of pearlized beads. The effect is pure Christmas magic.

SNOW WHITE
Wind Christmas lights and a shimmering silver ribbon in and out of the branches, working from the top down. Intersperse large white frosted baubles with shiny hearts, and add smaller silver balls in mirrored and etched glass to finish.

Artificial tree suits white and silver decorations

Large frosted bauble

Use white Christmas lights to highlight your favorite baubles

Twist silver wire-edged ribbon around the tree

Terracotta pot sprayed silver and edged with a garland of silver beads

Top the tree with
a glittery star and
frosted glass grapes

Decorated shell
(see page 27)

Hang large sequin
baubles (see page 26)
on the tree first

FROSTED TWIG TREE
*Spray a twig tree silver and contrast
sparkling silver baubles with creamy
sequin-covered globes. Fill empty branches
with lustrous polished shells on silver braid,
small gleaming glass baubles, and chandelier
droplets reminiscent of slippery icicles.*

Use small baubles
to fill in gaps

Brass-edged
mother-of-pearl disc

Bauble suspended
from rope of
pearly beads

Twig tree comes
with its own stand

PEARLY DECORATIONS

IN THE MONTHS BEFORE CHRISTMAS, start collecting sequins in shades of silver and cream, old pearl bead necklaces, fancy braid, shiny silver ribbons, and highly polished seashells to turn into gleaming decorations. Buy foam balls from craft stores and mix their round shapes with the elegance of long chandelier droplets for a stunning winter white Christmas tree.

SEQUIN BAUBLE Ingredients

◆ EQUIPMENT ◆

Darning needle

Glue

Foam ball, 8in (20cm)
in circumference

8in (20cm) bead trim

200 pearly sequins   50 silver sequins

250 pins

4in (10cm) silver cord

DECORATED SHELL Ingredients

2¾in (7cm)
polished shell

8in (20cm) string
pearl beads

2 small
pearl beads

4in (10cm) silver cord

◆ EQUIPMENT ◆

Glue

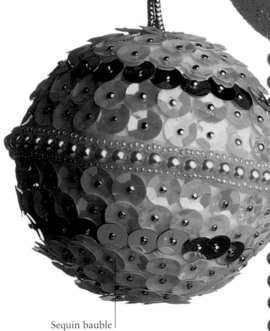

Sequin bauble
(see page 26)

String of beads used
to suspend bauble

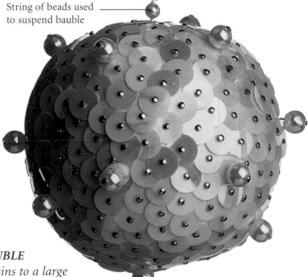

IRIDESCENT SEQUIN BAUBLE
Pin masses of gleaming sequins to a large
cotton ball and add a smattering of round
pearl beads to decorate.

Chandelier droplet
hanging from
decorated shell

Mirrored bauble reflects the light

Wire-edged organza ribbon

BAUBLE AND BOW
Tie silver wire-edged ribbon in a bow on top of a small pearly bauble decorated with dots of glitter.

Abalone shell with natural holes, from a shell shop

Polished shell wrapped with beads (see page 27)

ICICLE PENDANTS
Contrast an opaque patterned glass bauble on silver braid with graceful glass droplets.

SHINING SHELLS
Look in shell shops for shells polished until the underlying mother-of-pearl shows through.

Silver sequin bauble (see page 26)

MAKING THE SEQUIN BAUBLE

Stick to one or two simple colors of sequins, or experiment with alternating bands in vibrant colors. Wrapping strings of jazzy beads around the bauble adds glamor. WARNING: pinned sequin baubles can be dangerous for young children and animals.

1 Glue the bead trim horizontally around the center of the foam ball, making sure the trim is straight.

2 Working upward from the bead trim, push pins one by one through the center of the pearly sequins to secure them to the foam ball in two neat, slightly overlapping rings.

 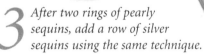 

3 After two rings of pearly sequins, add a row of silver sequins using the same technique.

4 Continue pinning on rings of pearl sequins until you reach the top of the ball, but do not cover the hole at the top. Repeat steps 2 through 4, working down from the bead trim.

5 Make a hole in the top of the ball with a darning needle and squeeze some glue into it. Make a loop of silver cord and push the ends into the hole to finish.

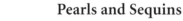

Pearls and Sequins

Studded Pearl Bauble
Cover a foam ball completely with pearl sequins, then pin a few pearl beads on top of the sequins. Hang from a string of pearls.

Silver Sequin Bauble
Divide a foam ball into quarters with four lines of pearl beads pinned in position, then fill in the quarters with silver sequins.

Silver sequin bauble

Studded pearl bauble

Making the Shell Decoration

Choose shells that have been polished until the underlying mother-of-pearl shows through. Although ideally suited to spiral-shaped shells and strings of pearls, this simple method can be adapted for any type of shells or beads.

1 Glue one end of the string of pearl beads to the edge of the hole in the top of the shell. Let it dry.

Small bead hides juncture of cord and beads

2 Wind the string of beads around the natural spiral of the shell, gluing it as you work. Cut the string when you reach the bottom.

3 Use strong glue to attach a small bead to the bottom of the shell so it covers the end of the string of beads. Let it dry.

4 Fold the silver cord into a loop and glue it inside the top of the shell. Cover the ends with a small bead.

Decorated Shells

Limpet Shell
Use the same technique on a conical shell and suspend from a looped string of pearl beads.

Translucent Disc
Glue tiny silver stars to a brass-edged mother-of-pearl disc and attach to silver cord threaded with pearl beads and a silver spiral.

Abalone Shell
Suspend a glass droplet from a piece of cord threaded through the holes of an abalone shell.

Pearly Disc
Glue small pearly beads to a mother-of-pearl disc and thread onto silver cord.

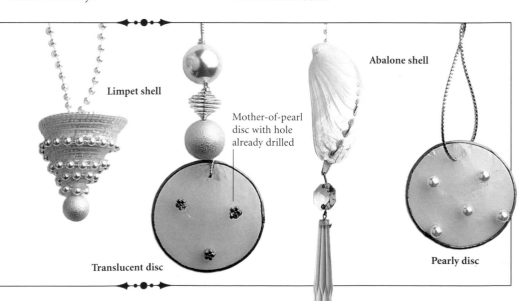

Limpet shell

Mother-of-pearl disc with hole already drilled

Abalone shell

Translucent disc

Pearly disc

COUNTRY-STYLE TREES

REJOICE IN ALL THINGS NATURAL at Christmastime, decking your tree out with flower petals, rich spices, ornate carved fruit, raffia baubles, and rosebuds, all bathed in the natural glow of candlelight. For something completely different, suspend golden pears from a variegated holly tree, and perch a fat gold partridge in a raffia nest among the branches.

PARTRIDGE IN A PEAR TREE
For a quirky take on the well-known Christmas carol, perch a golden partridge in a red raffia nest among the branches of a traditional holly tree. Golden pears hanging from the lowest branches complete the look.

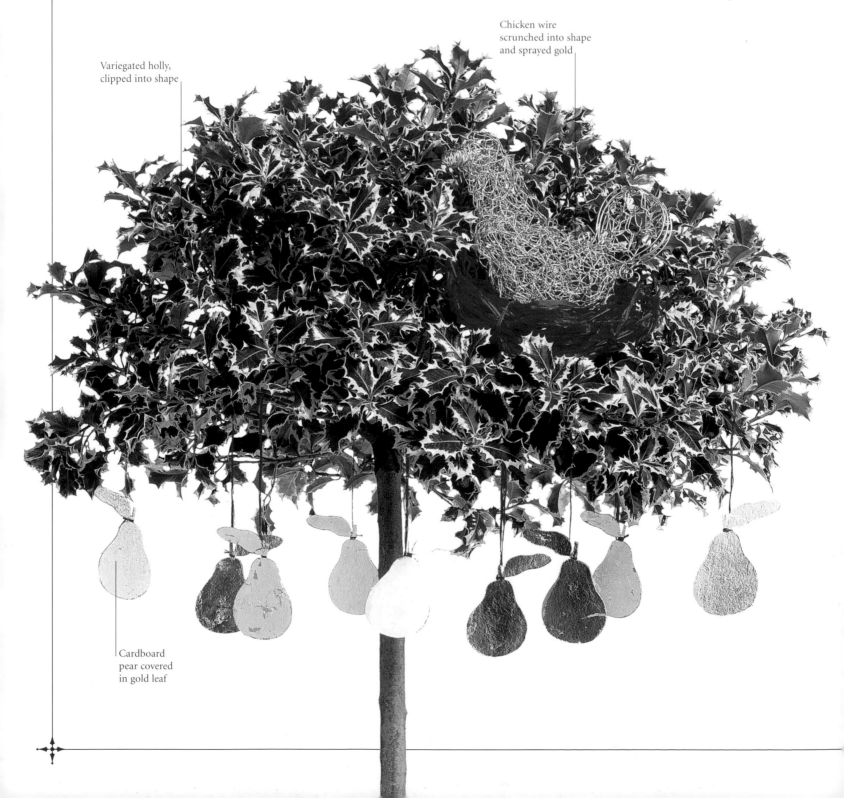

Variegated holly, clipped into shape

Chicken wire scrunched into shape and sprayed gold

Cardboard pear covered in gold leaf

FRUIT, SPICE, AND ALL THINGS NICE
*Fill the room with fragrance by gluing
aromatic spices, such as star anise, and small
chilies to foam balls, and by using dried
oranges, rose petals, and bunches of oregano
as decorations. Echo the deep green of a
Nordman fir with soft green candles and
complete the earthy theme with a woven
cane basket.*

Wooden animal shape
covered in a light
dusting of chalk

Green wax candles
for decoration

Dried orange
bauble (see page 31)

String bauble
echoes the
natural theme

Flower ball
(see page 30)

MAKING THE FLOWER BALL

Dried roses are ideal for making flower balls because the petals are slightly flexible and quite flat and retain much of their color when dried. Carefully open the petals and glue them so the best side faces outward.

Ingredients

10 dried roses per ball

Foam ball, 8in (20cm) in circumference

Medium-gauge floral wire

◆ EQUIPMENT ◆

Darning needle

Glue

1 *Gently pull the petals from the roses, making sure they are not damaged in the process. Discard imperfect petals.*

2 *Starting at the bottom of the ball, glue the petals on one by one so they form a slightly overlapping ring.*

Slightly overlap each ring of petals to hide the yellow tops

3 *Continue gluing the petals on, working around the ball toward the top, creating neat rings of petals.*

4 *When the ball is completely covered, use a darning needle to make a hole in the top. Fill it with glue and push in a piece of floral wire. To finish, bend the wire into a hook for hanging.*

Spicy Balls

Use the same technique to make baubles covered with tiny dried chilies, adzuki beans, or dried star anise, which fills the room with a lovely aroma.

Dried chilies

Adzuki beans

Dried star anise

MAKING THE CITRUS BAUBLES

The thick skin of oranges lends itself well to carving, so practice on them before attempting the thinner skin of limes. For perfectly dried baubles, choose very fresh, unwaxed produce and leave somewhere warm and dry for about two weeks.

Ingredients

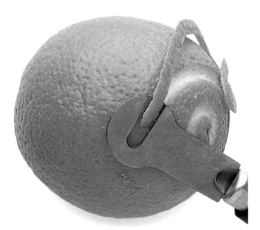

Fresh, unwaxed citrus fruit

Thick-gauge floral wires

◆ EQUIPMENT ◆

Canelle knife

Darning needle

Glue

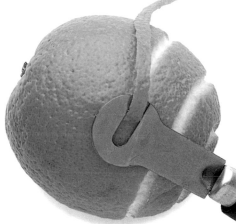

1 Use a canelle knife to start carving a spiral pattern into the skin of a plump, round, unwaxed orange.

2 Slowly continue the spiral until it reaches the bottom of the orange. If the peel breaks, start again from that point. Carve different patterns into other fruit (see inset) to make an entire set.

Ready to dry

Dried

3 Leave the fruit somewhere warm to dry for about two weeks. Any dampness in the atmosphere will ruin the baubles.

4 Make a hole in the top of the orange with a needle, glue a floral wire in the hole, and bend into a hook to finish.

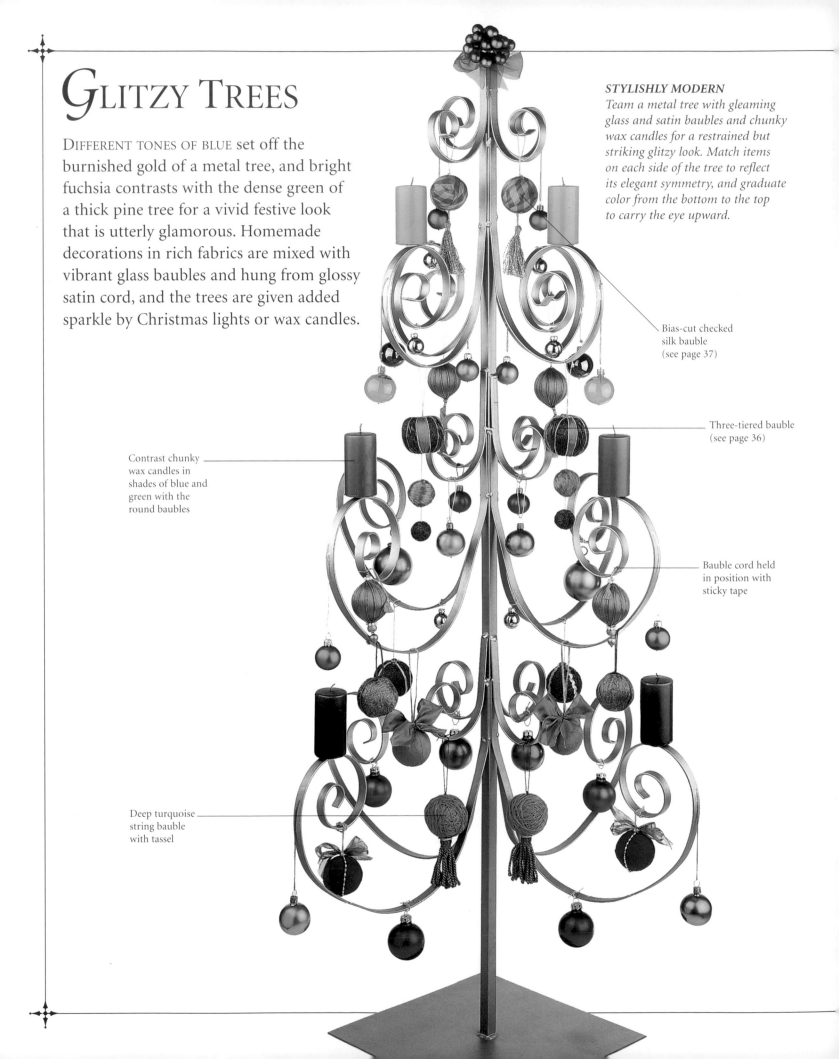

GLITZY TREES

DIFFERENT TONES OF BLUE set off the burnished gold of a metal tree, and bright fuchsia contrasts with the dense green of a thick pine tree for a vivid festive look that is utterly glamorous. Homemade decorations in rich fabrics are mixed with vibrant glass baubles and hung from glossy satin cord, and the trees are given added sparkle by Christmas lights or wax candles.

STYLISHLY MODERN
Team a metal tree with gleaming glass and satin baubles and chunky wax candles for a restrained but striking glitzy look. Match items on each side of the tree to reflect its elegant symmetry, and graduate color from the bottom to the top to carry the eye upward.

Bias-cut checked silk bauble (see page 37)

Three-tiered bauble (see page 36)

Contrast chunky wax candles in shades of blue and green with the round baubles

Bauble cord held in position with sticky tape

Deep turquoise string bauble with tassel

PINK, PURPLE, AND GOLD
Load a Scots pine tree with dazzling colored glass baubles, raw silk pouches, shiny foil crackers, and tiny wrapped gifts nestling in the branches. Scatter golden garlands throughout; add multicolored Christmas lights and place a theatrical star on top to steal the limelight.

Shiny silk string
baubles dotted
randomly on tree

Rest tiny foil
crackers on the
bushy branches

Pouch made
from luxurious silk
saturated in color

Mauve-blue basket
tied with cerise ribbon

Christmas light
shines on the
gold star

Tiny gift wrapped
in shiny paper

Layer of moss
covers damp soil

FABRIC BAUBLES

WIND SHIMMERING FABRICS AND TRIMMINGS in jewel-like colors around lightweight foam balls to make sumptuous tree decorations and add textural contrast to the extravagant display with store-bought glass and spangled baubles. Break up their strong outlines with iridescent ribbons twisted into bows, and suspend your opulent creations from lengths of colored tinsel ribbon and glittering braid, silk yarn, and gold cord.

THREE-TIERED BAUBLE Ingredients

Foam ball, 8in (20cm) in circumference

Foam ball, 4in (10cm) in circumference

5¹⁄₂yd (5m) knitting yarn

Three colored knitting yarns, 8¹⁄₂yd (8m) each

Foam ball, 3in (8cm) in circumference

◆ EQUIPMENT ◆

Tweezers

Darning needle

Fabric glue

¹⁄₂yd (0.5m) thick gold rope

3¹⁄₄yd (3m) thin twisted gold cord

5¹⁄₂yd (5m) knitting yarn

CHECKED SILK BAUBLE Ingredients

¹⁄₂yd (0.5m) gold cord

Store-bought gold tassel

◆ EQUIPMENT ◆

Dressmaking pins

Fabric scissors

Iron

Fabric glue

Silk, ¹⁄₂ x ¹⁄₂yd (0.5 x 0.5m)

T-pin

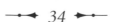

Foam ball, 8in (20cm) in circumference

GOLD GLITTER BALL
Soften the effect of a store-bought gold bauble with a delicate gold and turquoise voile bow.

Glittering theatrical tassel

CHECKED SILK BAUBLE
Wrap thin strips of gleaming checked silk haphazardly around a ball for a rich, vibrant effect. An oversized gold tassel provides a bold splash of glitter.

GLASS BAUBLES
Combine metallic glass baubles with fabric decorations.

JADE BALL
Set jade dupion silk against an elegant green voile bow.

Sparking gold cord connects each ball

THREE-TIERED BAUBLE
Wrap silky blue, purple, and multicolored yarns around three balls. Use gold cord to highlight the colored segments and lead the eye through the decoration.

PLUM BALL
Wind vivid purple yarn onto a ball and enhance it with a wire-edged bow and gold braid.

GREEN AND PURPLE BAUBLE
Thread emerald green and deep purple knitting yarns through a foam ball to create solid blocks of color edged with gold braid. Secure blue tinsel ribbon to the bauble with a T-pin.

MAKING THE THREE-TIERED BAUBLE

First make a hole in the large foam ball (see inset below). Then divide each of the three 8½yd (8m) lengths of yarn into quarters before threading them through the hole. Yarns are wound onto the small balls and glued.

1 Thread one piece of blue yarn on a needle, pass it through the hole in the large ball, and tie it to form a loop.

2 Twist the knot into the hole to conceal it and continue threading the yarn through the ball, as shown, creating a segment of color. Secure the end by hooking it under previous turns of yarn.

3 Repeat with one piece of purple yarn, then one piece of multicolored yarn. Alternate the colors until the ball is covered. Then thread 3yd (2.75m) of thin gold cord around each segment. Secure as before.

4 Wind a length of purple yarn around the small ball and a length of blue yarn around the medium ball.

Secure the loose end of yarn with glue

5 With a darning needle, pull the rest of the gold cord through the smaller balls. Between each two balls, make a knot and leave 1in (2.5cm) of cord. Glue the cord into the hole at the bottom of the large ball.

Leave 1in (2.5cm) of gold cord between each ball

Dab glue in the top of the hole

Making a hole in a ball

Using a darning needle, carefully make a tiny hole in a foam ball. Gradually increase the width of the hole with a small knife. Then work from the other end of the ball in the same way until the hole is about 1in (2.5cm) wide all through the ball.

6 Glue a 2½in (6cm) piece of gold rope around the top of the hole in the large ball. Knot one end of the remaining rope and glue it into the hole. Tie the other end of the rope to the tree.

MAKING THE CHECKED SILK BAUBLE

Start by cutting the silk on the bias (see inset steps below), to create thin strips that mold themselves easily around the circular foam shape. The number of strips you use depends on how you wrap them on the ball.

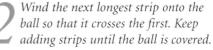

Wrap the second strip across the first

Cutting strips on the bias

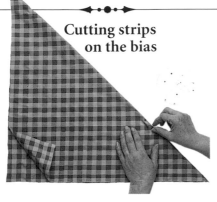

1 Fold the square of silk diagonally in half to locate the longest bias line. Place pins along this folded edge at ⅜in (1cm) intervals.

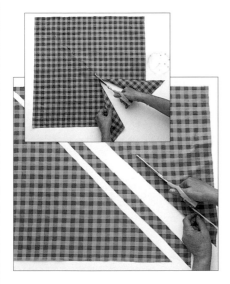

2 Open up the square and cut along the bias, removing the pins as you go. Continue to cut each half of silk into 1⅜in (3.5cm) wide strips.

3 Turn the raw edges of the strips over and pin to the wrong side of the silk. Press them with an iron, removing the pins, to create a neat finish.

1 Wrap the longest strip of silk around the ball, securing the end by overlapping it with the next turn of fabric.

2 Wind the next longest strip onto the ball so that it crosses the first. Keep adding strips until the ball is covered.

Push the T-pin through the end of silk

3 Secure the last strip with a T-pin. Hook a loop of gold cord with knotted ends under the pin for hanging.

4 Push a pin through the top of the tassel, dab glue on the pinhead, and push it into the bottom of the ball.

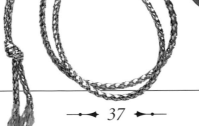

EDIBLE TREES

A CHRISTMAS TREE CREAKING under the weight of delicious-looking edible decorations is a delight to the eye as well as the palate. Choose a natural color scheme using cookies and dried fruit, or pander to the children of the house with a tempting mix of colored candies, lollipops, wrapped chocolates, and net bags of gold-wrapped chocolate coins.

CONFECTIONERY DELIGHT

For a tree that is a guaranteed hit with children, twist wire around the ends of wrapped candies to make long garlands, and bundle small candies into squares of cellophane tied with colorful cord. Attach brightly wrapped candies and lollipops with pieces of wire and set the whole tree ablaze with red Christmas lights.

Candy cane hooked
over branch

Colored candies in
cellophane packets

Garland of
wrapped chocolates
twisted on wire

Quirky vegetable-
shaped baubles

Tie long pieces of
marshmallow to the
tree with ribbon

Sacks of gold
coins placed
randomly

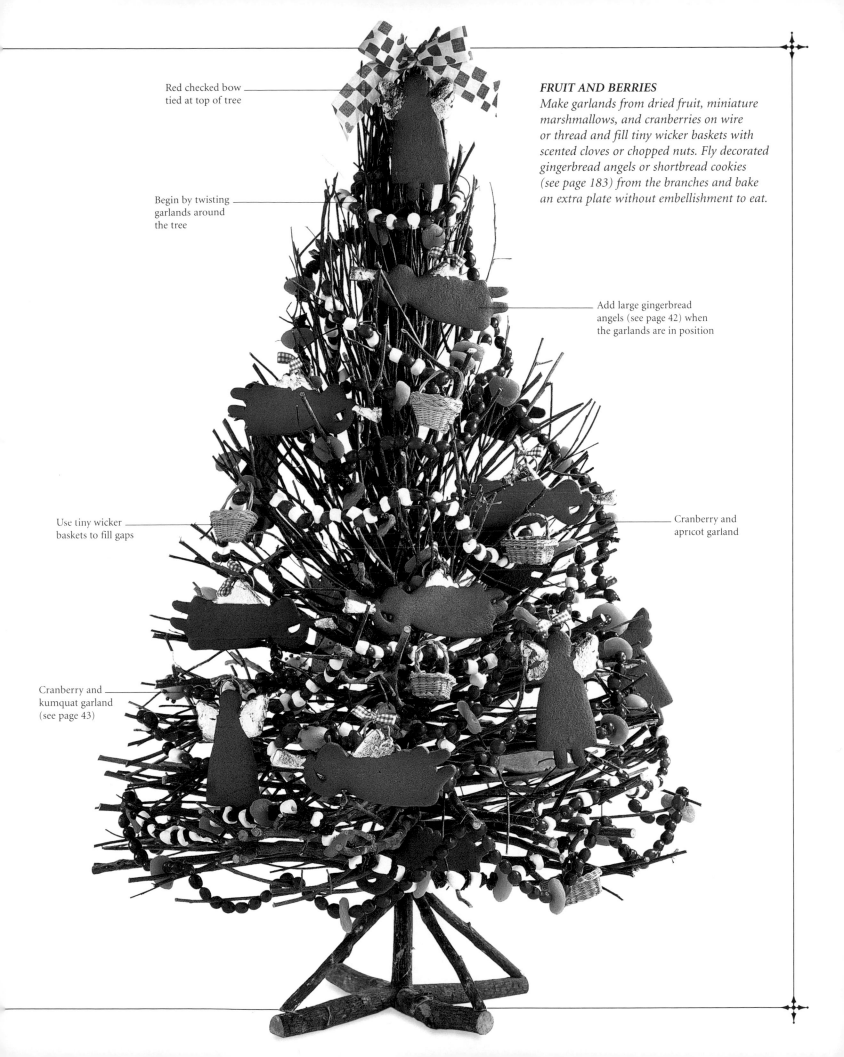

Red checked bow
tied at top of tree

Begin by twisting
garlands around
the tree

Use tiny wicker
baskets to fill gaps

Cranberry and
kumquat garland
(see page 43)

FRUIT AND BERRIES
*Make garlands from dried fruit, miniature
marshmallows, and cranberries on wire
or thread and fill tiny wicker baskets with
scented cloves or chopped nuts. Fly decorated
gingerbread angels or shortbread cookies
(see page 183) from the branches and bake
an extra plate without embellishment to eat.*

Add large gingerbread
angels (see page 42) when
the garlands are in position

Cranberry and
apricot garland

EDIBLE TREE DECORATIONS

FOR DECORATIVE FESTIVE garlands, thread shiny cranberries and kumquats studded with aromatic cloves onto wire, or alternate dried cherries, apricot slices, and miniature marshmallows. Suspend gingerbread angels with golden wings from gold rings trimmed with ribbon, and bake an unadorned batch for eating (one recipe makes ten angels).

GINGERBREAD ANGEL Ingredients

SAFETY FIRST
Do not eat angels with rings glued to them; bake a separate plate for eating.

1 recipe gingerbread dough (see page 181)

White of egg, optional

10 curtain rings

59in (150cm) gold thread

Pad of gold leaf (optional)

1yd (1m) checked ribbon

◆ EQUIPMENT ◆

Paper	Wire rack
Pencil	Bowl (optional)
Scissors	
Flour, to dust	Egg whisk (optional)
Rolling pin	
Kitchen knife	Fine paintbrush (optional)
Nonstick baking parchment	Spoon
Baking tray	Glue

CRANBERRY GARLAND Ingredients

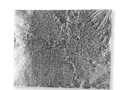

5 kumquats

50 cloves

70 cranberries per 1yd (1m) wire

Medium-gauge floral wire

◆ EQUIPMENT ◆

Wire cutters

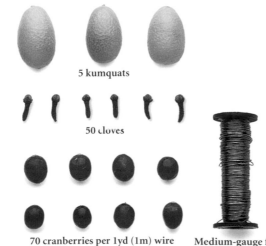

Wicker basket filled with cloves

NATURAL COLORS
Give decorations a natural feel using the muted colors of dried fruit, cloves, wicker baskets, gingerbread, and gingham ribbon, and brighten the effect with fresh kumquats.

Marshmallows and
cranberries strung
in a garland

Marshmallows,
threaded with
alternating dried
apricot slices and
dried cherries

Cranberries and
dried apricot slices

Cranberry garland adorned
with kumquats (see page 43)

Flying angel (see page
188 for template)

MAKING THE GINGERBREAD ANGELS

For ten angels, make up one recipe of gingerbread following steps 1 and 2 of the Gingerbread House recipe on page 181. If you do not wish to use gold leaf, decorate with colored icing or gold paste from a cake-decorating store instead.

Reroll the dough to get ten neat angels

1 *Copy the angel template on page 188 onto paper and cut it out. Mix the gingerbread dough and roll it out on a lightly floured surface to a thickness of about ¼in (6mm).*

2 *Place the paper angel on the dough and cut around it with a small kitchen knife. Repeat to make ten angels.*

3 *Line a baking tray with nonstick kitchen parchment and lay the gingerbread angels carefully on it. Bake at 375°F/190°C for 8-10 minutes, until firm. Cool on a wire rack.*

4 *If using gold leaf, lightly whisk the white of an egg and paint it onto the angel's wings with a fine paintbrush. Otherwise decorate the angel as desired and add the ring and bow as directed in step 6.*

Gold leaf applied by rubbing with back of spoon

5 *Tear a sheet of gold leaf and its backing from a pad. Cut a piece the size of the angel's wing and position it on the wing. Rub the backing with the back of a spoon to apply the transfer.*

6 *Peel the backing off and repeat with the other wing. To finish, glue a gold ring to the back of the angel's head. Tie a small bow to the top of the curtain ring with gold thread and hang from a long loop of gold thread.*

MAKING THE CRANBERRY GARLAND

Fresh red cranberries interspersed with kumquats make ideal decorative garlands and remain attractive when dried. Miniature marshmallows, dried fruit slices, cherries, and figs strung on thread make delicious edible garlands.

1 *Push the cloves one by one into the kumquats to form a ring around the middle of each fruit.*

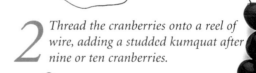

2 *Thread the cranberries onto a reel of wire, adding a studded kumquat after nine or ten cranberries.*

3 *Continue threading cranberries and kumquats until the garland is the desired length. To finish, bend large loops in the ends of the wire to prevent the fruit from sliding off the ends.*

CARNIVAL TREES

HOT, RIOTOUS COLORS bring instant warmth and sunshine indoors for Christmas. Golden suns, vibrant tinplate shapes, dazzling baubles, and long garlands of paper beads almost hide the branches of a Norwegian spruce, and vividly colored miniature citrus fruits nestle among the glossy green leaves of a bay tree.

TIE A YELLOW RIBBON
Wire tiny citrus-colored bows to kumquats and small limes and scatter them evenly throughout the leaves of a bushy bay tree. Match the bows with a lemon yellow ribbon spiraled around the trunk.

Cheat's bow (see page 105) attached to small lime and fixed to branch with wire

Thick yellow ribbon wound around trunk

FESTIVE FUN

Crowd a Norwegian spruce with masses of paper, tin, and glass decorations in the craziest colors possible. Fill spaces with jazzy baubles, snake a garland of paper beads through the branches, and add multicolored Christmas lights to finish.

Tinplate fish
(see page 46)

Aztec-style sun

Multicolored
paper bead garland
(see page 47)

MAKING THE TINPLATE FISH

Check your telephone directory for suppliers of sheets of
tinplate and choose a thin sheet that is easy to cut.
To avoid damaging the table top when punching patterns
into tinplate, use a piece of thick cardboard as a base.

◆ EQUIPMENT ◆

Sharp pencil

Cardboard

Craft knife

Cutting mat

Old scissors

Thick card

Nail

Hammer

Hole punch

Ingredients

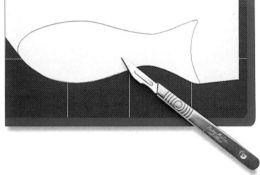

Tinplate, 6½ x 2⅓in (16 x 6cm)

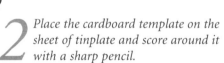

Felt-tip pens

6in (15cm) cord

1 Copy the fish template on page 186
onto a piece of cardboard; cut it out
carefully with a scalpel.

2 Place the cardboard template on the
sheet of tinplate and score around it
with a sharp pencil.

3 Use old, blunt scissors to cut
carefully around the scored line,
making sure there are no jagged edges.

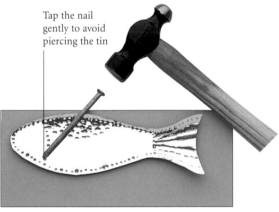

Tap the nail
gently to avoid
piercing the tin

4 Place the tinplate fish on a piece of thick
cardboard; use a nail and hammer to
punch a pattern on the shiny side.

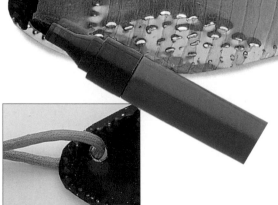

5 Use colored felt-tip pens
to decorate the shiny side
of the fish. Pierce one end
with a hole punch and thread a
piece of cord through it to hang
(see inset).

MAKING THE PAPER BEAD GARLAND

Start amassing pieces of scrap paper – most types can be used to make these beads as long as they are brightly colored. Thick paper will make heavy, bulky beads, and thinner paper will make more refined and delicate beads.

Ingredients

Selection of colored papers,
18 x 13⅚in (45 x 35cm)

2yd (1.8m)
colored cord

◆ EQUIPMENT ◆

Craft glue

Paintbrush

3 garden stakes,
20in (50cm) long

Sharp knife

1 Brush craft glue onto the reverse of one piece of colored paper, leaving about 3in (7.5cm) at the bottom without any glue.

2 Lay the stake across the end of the unpasted section of paper and roll the paper tightly around it. When you reach the end of the paper, leave the stake in place while the glue dries to prevent warping. Repeat with the other sheets of colored paper.

3 When the glue is dry, use a sharp knife to slice the paper tube into 1in (2.5cm) beads. Leave the stake in place while slicing to prevent the beads from being squashed in the process.

4 Measure out a piece of cord as long as you want the garland to be. Thread the beads onto it one by one, tying the string in a loop around the bead at each end of the garland to secure.

WREATHS, GARLANDS, & FLOWERS

*Glossy evergreen leaves and colorful
berries have always symbolized the hope
of new life in the depths of a northern winter.
Use them in combination with fresh or dried
flowers, fruit, and nuts to make seasonal
wreaths, garlands, and door swags that
will transform your home into the
essence of Christmas hospitality.*

FESTIVE GREEN WREATH

AN EXTRAVAGANT WREATH on the front door gives guests a hint of the seasonal festivities to be enjoyed inside the house, and this unusual wreath is large enough to adorn any outside door. Be a little different with a homemade diamond-shaped base, and use an eye-catching mix of fresh and dried leaves, flowers, and fruit, brightened for Christmas with shiny baubles in shades of blue and green. To finish, draw the eye to the center with two lavish bauble-trimmed bows made from thick green ribbons edged in gold.

FESTIVE GREEN WREATH Ingredients

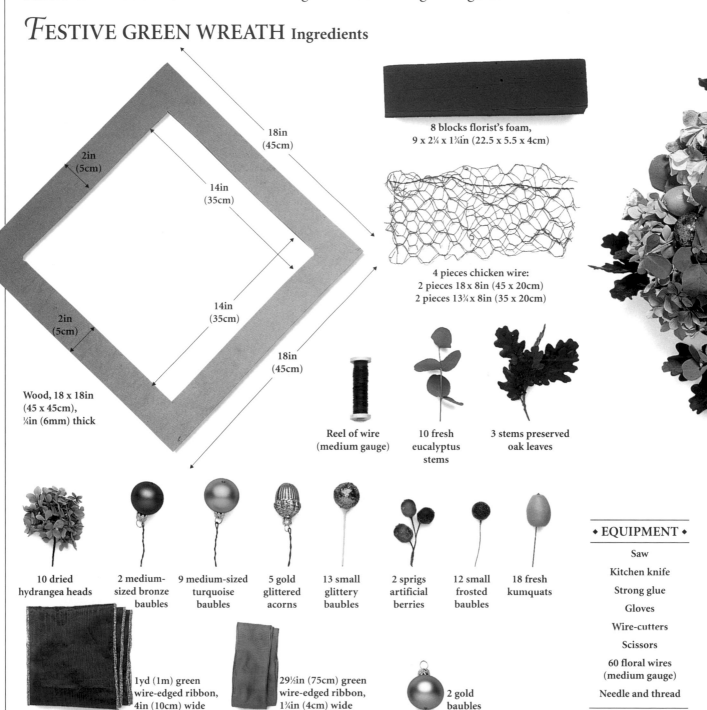

18in (45cm)

2in (5cm)

14in (35cm)

14in (35cm)

2in (5cm)

18in (45cm)

Wood, 18 x 18in (45 x 45cm), ¼in (6mm) thick

8 blocks florist's foam, 9 x 2¼ x 1¾in (22.5 x 5.5 x 4cm)

4 pieces chicken wire: 2 pieces 18 x 8in (45 x 20cm) 2 pieces 13¾ x 8in (35 x 20cm)

Reel of wire (medium gauge)

10 fresh eucalyptus stems

3 stems preserved oak leaves

10 dried hydrangea heads

2 medium-sized bronze baubles

9 medium-sized turquoise baubles

5 gold glittered acorns

13 small glittery baubles

2 sprigs artificial berries

12 small frosted baubles

18 fresh kumquats

1yd (1m) green wire-edged ribbon, 4in (10cm) wide

29½in (75cm) green wire-edged ribbon, 1¾in (4cm) wide

2 gold baubles

◆ EQUIPMENT ◆

Saw

Kitchen knife

Strong glue

Gloves

Wire-cutters

Scissors

60 floral wires (medium gauge)

Needle and thread

Fresh kumquats
add color

Small pieces
of hydrangea
fill in gaps

MAKING THE WREATH

Before you start, break the hydrangea heads, eucalyptus, and oak leaves into small sprigs, and cut natural stems quite short. Slip pieces of floral wire into kumquats, and twist them through the top of the baubles, so they can be easily secured in the foam.

Chicken wire covers florist's
foam completely and wraps
around to the back

Blocks of florist's
foam cut to fit frame

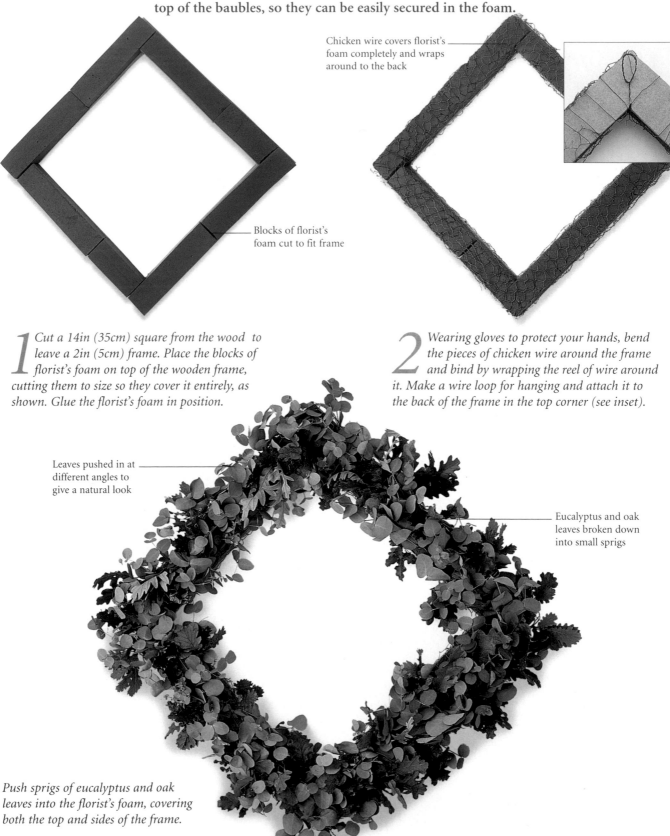

1 *Cut a 14in (35cm) square from the wood to leave a 2in (5cm) frame. Place the blocks of florist's foam on top of the wooden frame, cutting them to size so they cover it entirely, as shown. Glue the florist's foam in position.*

2 *Wearing gloves to protect your hands, bend the pieces of chicken wire around the frame and bind by wrapping the reel of wire around it. Make a wire loop for hanging and attach it to the back of the frame in the top corner (see inset).*

Leaves pushed in at
different angles to
give a natural look

Eucalyptus and oak
leaves broken down
into small sprigs

3 *Push sprigs of eucalyptus and oak leaves into the florist's foam, covering both the top and sides of the frame.*

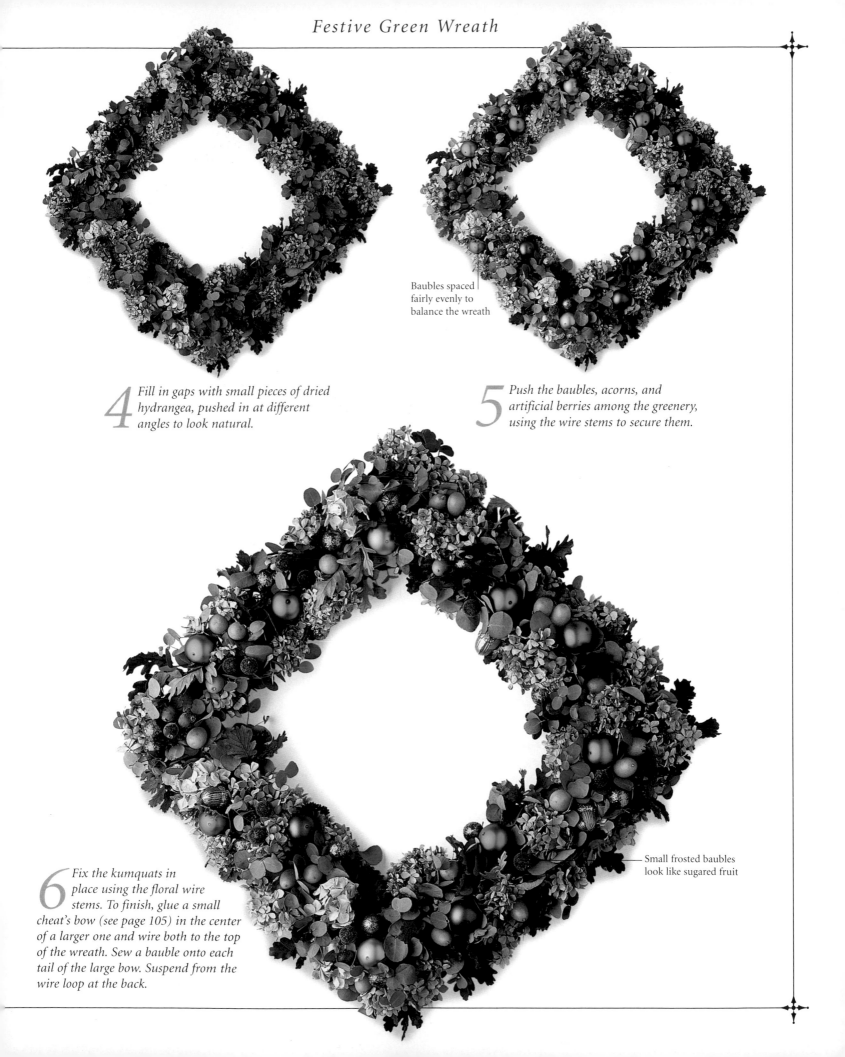

4 *Fill in gaps with small pieces of dried hydrangea, pushed in at different angles to look natural.*

Baubles spaced fairly evenly to balance the wreath

5 *Push the baubles, acorns, and artificial berries among the greenery, using the wire stems to secure them.*

6 *Fix the kumquats in place using the floral wire stems. To finish, glue a small cheat's bow (see page 105) in the center of a larger one and wire both to the top of the wreath. Sew a bauble onto each tail of the large bow. Suspend from the wire loop at the back.*

Small frosted baubles look like sugared fruit

DOOR SWAGS

A DOOR SWAG MAKES a stylish alternative to the traditional Christmas wreath, brightening up the house with festive glamor. For the front door, make a robust evergreen swag that will withstand harsh weather, and use dried flowers, scented spices, and pretty ribbons to make more delicate arrangements for doors inside the home.

BEECH TWIGS
Secure beech twigs in a bundle with wire, then tie the bundle with a red raffia bow. Wire tiny exotic fruits and raffia bows onto the branches and finish with a stuffed tree decoration.

EVERGREEN DROP
Starting at the bottom, wire bunches of blue spruce to a stake so that each layer slightly overlaps the one below. Add red glass grapes at the seams and tie two taffeta cheat's bows (see page 105) at the top.

FLORAL CORNET
Remove the leaves from a bunch of celosia and place it in a cone of chicken wire lined with damp moss. Squeeze it to secure the flowers, then cover by pinning on overlapping celosia leaves. Decorate with a spiral of gold braid and hang from a loop of ribbon.

Celosia leaves
pinned in place
with fine wire

Top edge of
leaves folded
neatly over

HOLLY AND IVY BUNCH
Make a flat bundle of blue spruce, holly, and ivy and wire it at the top, tying the bundle with a green taffeta ribbon. Decorate with cranberries threaded onto rings of floral wire.

Miniature wreath
made of cranberries

DRIED SWAG
Adorn the front of a store-bought twig-and-spruce swag with cinnamon sticks, dried hydrangea, an artichoke sprayed gold, and artificial apples. Wire or glue the items in place and finish with a glossy double bow (see page 105).

GARLANDS

BRING THE DELIGHTS of the garden indoors for festive celebrations by making a bountiful Christmas garland for the house. Create a garland with drop swags to fit around a doorway or window arch, lay a long garland down the center of the dining table, or entwine it around stair banisters for sheer flamboyance.

Sparkling artificial berries wired to the center of bows

Double bows in contrasting russet and gold ribbons

GILDED GARLAND

Cover a store-bought drop swag garland of overlapping bay leaves with gilding creme and twist a russet rope around the main section. Decorate the swags with double bows made using contrasting wire-edged ribbons (see page 105).

Pecans wired to the rope

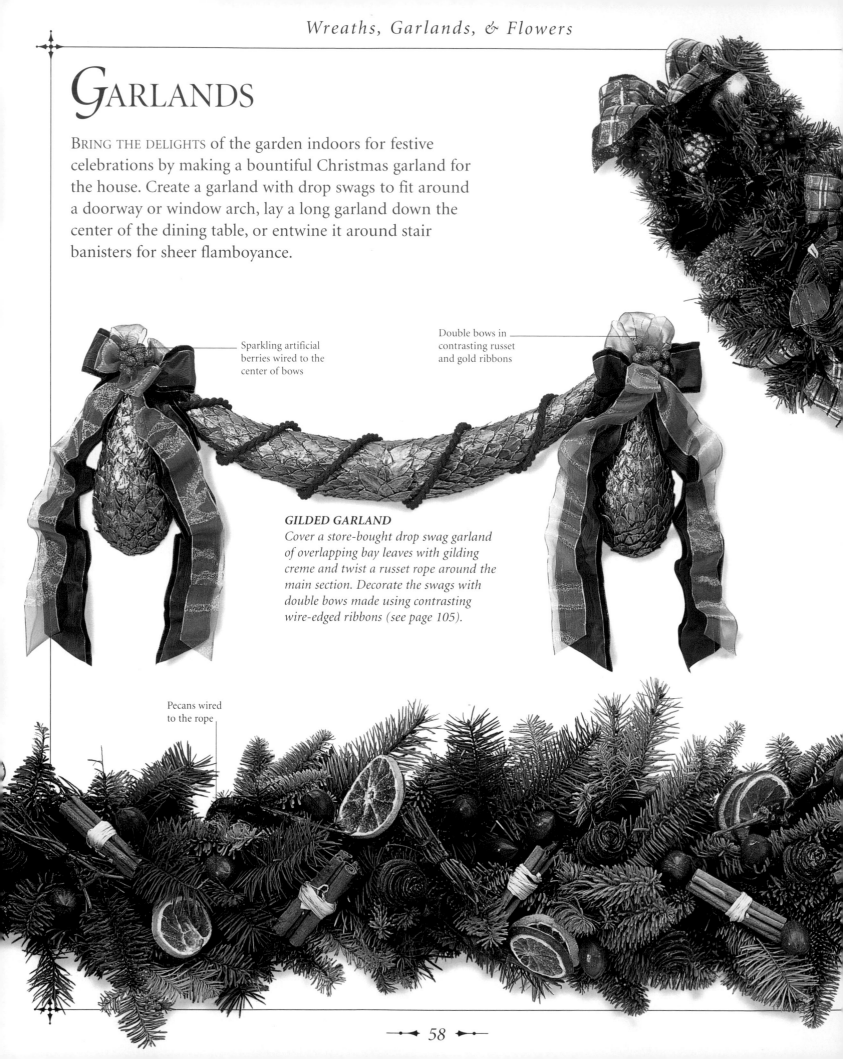

Store-bought
bark apples

FESTIVE FIR SWAG
*Decorate an artificial fir swag by wiring to
it gold-sprayed dried fruit, nuts, and seeds,
apples made from tree bark, artificial cones,
nuts, and berries. Finish with bows made
from wire-edged ribbon.*

SPRUCE AND SPICE
*Wire sprigs of blue spruce onto
a thick rope that is easy to drape
around furniture. Cover it with
wired pecans, cones, dried chilies,
and orange slices, and bunches of
twigs and cinnamon sticks.*

FRUIT GARLAND

PACK A LUSCIOUS GARLAND with festive evergreens, fresh red apples, carved dried citrus fruit (see page 31), dried pomegranates and wired pecans, and add sophistication with shimmering wire-edged ribbons in gold-green and burgundy.

FRUIT GARLAND Ingredients

— 43in (110cm) —

Twig frame

18in
(45cm)

Drop swags

Chicken wire,
59 x 8in (150 x 20cm)

Small bag of
fresh moss

Reel of fine
floral wire

8 bamboo sticks,
10in (25cm)

Fresh red apples add
color and shine

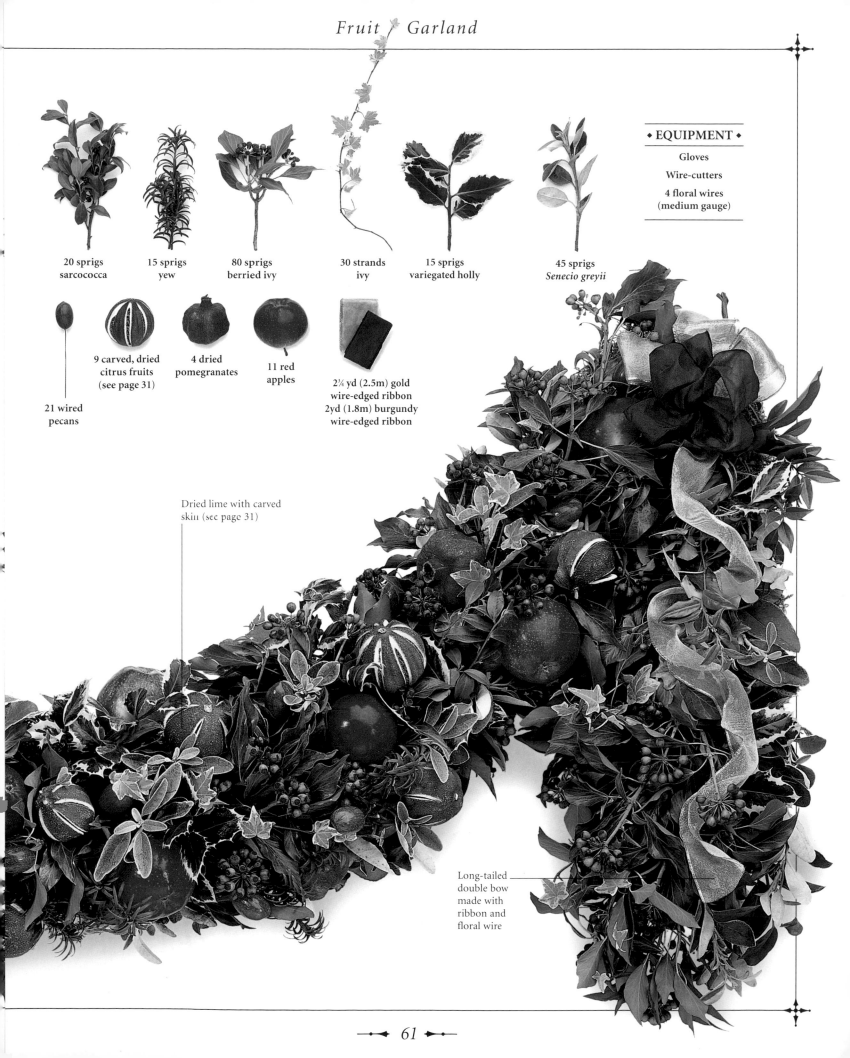

20 sprigs
sarcococca

15 sprigs
yew

80 sprigs
berried ivy

30 strands
ivy

15 sprigs
variegated holly

45 sprigs
Senecio greyii

◆ EQUIPMENT ◆

Gloves

Wire-cutters

4 floral wires
(medium gauge)

9 carved, dried
citrus fruits
(see page 31)

4 dried
pomegranates

11 red
apples

2¾ yd (2.5m) gold
wire-edged ribbon
2yd (1.8m) burgundy
wire-edged ribbon

21 wired
pecans

Dried lime with carved
skin (see page 31)

Long-tailed
double bow
made with
ribbon and
floral wire

TOPIARY TREES

COLLECT A CLUSTER of miniature topiary trees in varying shapes and colors for an original Christmas display. A tiny conical evergreen topped with a majestic purple bauble mimics a Christmas tree, while a larger ball of holly and berried ivy sits on top of deliciously scented cinnamon sticks. Dried hydrangea heads, gold balls, and pink paper flowers make a lasting arrangement that contrasts well with the glossy density of evergreens.

MAKING A TOPIARY TREE

Ingredients

Block florist's foam, 13½ x 4 x 3¼in (34 x 10 x 8cm)

Pot, 5⅛in (14cm) tall

4 branches boxwood

Small bauble

10in (25cm) bamboo stick

◆ EQUIPMENT ◆

Kitchen knife

1 floral wire (medium gauge)

Flat square surface for bauble at top of pyramid

Boxwood sprigs pushed together to hide foam

1 Cut a block of florist's foam into two pieces, each 4 x 4 x 3¼in (10 x 10 x 8cm). Place one on top of the other and push the bamboo stick through both of them. Use a kitchen knife to cut the foam into a four-sided pyramid, leaving a small flat surface at the top.

2 Cut the remaining foam to fit the pot, and put it inside. Set the pyramid on top, using the bamboo stick to secure.

3 Break the branches of boxwood into tiny sprigs and, starting at the bottom, push them one by one into the foam pyramid so no foam shows.

4 Gradually build up the boxwood sprigs until the foam is completely covered. To finish, slip a wire through the loop on the bauble and push it into the flat surface of foam at the top.

HOLLY AND IVY SPHERE
Stand a bunch of long cinnamon sticks in a pot filled with dry florist's foam, and push a ball of damp florist's foam covered in sprigs of holly and berried ivy onto the cinnamon sticks. Cover the filled pot with a layer of velvety bun moss and decorate with a gold star and a scattering of tiny gifts.

PRETTY IN PINK
Push dried hydrangea heads, paper roses and gold papier-mâché balls on wires into dry florist's foam and wedge it into a pot. Finish with a lavish bow.

Cinnamon sticks
act as a stem

MINI TREE
Contrast shiny evergreen leaves with purple and matte gold for a regal look.

FESTIVE FLOWERS

FOR A FRESH TAKE ON Christmas decorations, try an eye-catching arrangement of flowers in traditional festive colors. Keep each arrangement simple in itself and, for maximum impact, group it with others that are different in height, size, color, and texture. Clever use of plain glass vases in interesting shapes allows the flowers to take center stage.

Classic display of red short-stemmed roses

Dense grouping of ranunculus, gerbera, red anemones, and poinsettia

White anemones cut down short to fit a small square tank

Fleshy stems of red
amaryllis stand
tall in a vase

Masses of juicy red
berries contrast
with round red
chilies on stems

Brussels sprouts and
Romanesco cauliflower
florets spiked on
bamboo sticks

Squash

Limequat or
other exotic fruit

Scented white
hyacinth (below)
embedded in a
tank of damp
moss

"Paper white" narcissi
tied with raffia

Vase lined with sprigs
of spruce, then filled
with florist's foam

KISSING BOUGH

THE CUSTOMARY EVERGREEN kissing bough is more than just a Christmas decoration: the juicy red apple in the center symbolizes plenty and fertility for the coming season. Hung by the door, the bunch of mistletoe means no visitor can avoid a Christmas kiss! Pack the globe with evergreens, wire brightly colored ribbons into bows, and add gilded fruit, baubles, and tiny Christmas tree decorations for extra-festive sparkle.

Bunch of mistletoe with stems wired and tied with a ribbon

KISSING BOUGH Ingredients

5½yd (5m) steel wire

Carpet tape

Reel of fine floral wire

Apple

1¼in (3cm) bamboo stick

8in (20cm) gold thread

20in (50cm) thick cord

20 strands ivy

Making wired ribbon bows

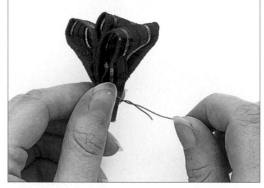

Zigzag 6in (15cm) of ribbon into three small loops and pinch the ends. Twist a short piece of floral wire around the pinched ends, leaving enough extra to act as a stem. Make 10 of these bows for the kissing bough.

2¼yd (2m) tartan ribbon

50 artificial berries

12 stems mistletoe

Red artificial berries
on wire stems

FORBIDDEN FRUIT
*Make the kissing bough
full to overflowing with
lush greenery, but ensure that
a tempting glimpse of the apple
can be caught between the boughs.*

FRUIT AND FLOWER DISPLAY

A MAGNIFICENT TOWER of spectacular fruit and flowers is guaranteed to turn a Christmas banquet into a feast for the eyes. Buy gilded walnuts on wires, twist floral wire through and around stems of roses and hypericum, and push it into litchis and berries in advance to secure them in the display.

FRUIT AND FLOWER DISPLAY Ingredients

Cone of florist's foam, 8in (20cm) base diameter, 20in (50cm) high

25 large handfuls loose moss

Reel of fine floral wire

31 bamboo sticks, 10in (25cm) long, broken into 92 lengths

8 plane leaves, sprayed gold

♦ EQUIPMENT ♦

Kitchen knife

140 floral wires (medium gauge)

15 red apples

25 persimmons

27 plums

14 small pears

42 roses

30 litchis

14 gilded walnuts

5 apricots

5 passion fruits

8 bunches hypericum

70 ivy leaves

60 cranberries

1 mini pineapple

MAKING THE DISPLAY

1 *Slice off the top 2½in (6cm) of the cone. Fasten the moss to the cone one handful at a time, wrapping the wire around it to secure.*

2 *Place the cone on a bed of gold plane leaves. Slipping short lengths of bamboo into the fruit as you work, push rings of skewered apples, persimmons, and plums into the foam. Build up the display by adding rings of small pears, roses, litchis, more persimmons, and plums.*

3 *Add more rings of gilded walnuts, apricots and passion fruits, litchis, roses, and hypericum. To finish, add cranberries to fill gaps, slide ivy leaves between the layers, and place the pineapple on a bamboo stick at the top.*

Pineapple
skewered in place

FESTIVE FRUIT
*Mix brightly colored fruit in
different sizes and textures with
a few gilded nuts and leaves for
special Christmas glitter.*

Hypericum
decorates the top
few layers

Ring of ivy
leaves slipped
between the layers

Cranberries interspersed
among larger fruit

CHRISTMAS LIGHTS & EFFECTS

*Lighting plays an important part in creating
the right atmosphere for a party, be it
old-fashioned candles smelling sweetly of beeswax,
bright modern candles in a bold candelabra, or
the romance of a chandelier made from twigs.
Let quirky lanterns swing enticingly in the porch,
beckoning guests inside where handmade
centerpieces and beautifully decorated mantelpieces
provide a focus for the season's festivities.*

AN ARRAY OF CANDLES

THE SOFT, FLICKERING LIGHT and evocative scent of a host of beautiful candles conjure up the ideal ambiance for a Christmas gathering. Choose from rolled beeswax, twisted, tapered, or square candles, the traditional church variety, molded novelties, or floating flowery candles in festive colors. Reflect the opulence of the season by adorning complementary candleholders with twisted ribbons, cords, and bows.

BEESWAX CANDLES

Choose exquisite beeswax candles for their natural texture and the delicious honey fragrance given off when they burn. Tie thin candles of differing heights together in small bundles to render candlesticks unnecessary.

FLOATING CANDLES

Make beautiful reflections with glittery flower-shaped candles floating in a wide-rimmed, shallow bowl. Scatter petals on the surface of the water for a truly luxurious feel.

Spiral candle decorated with a ring of sparkling glass droplets

Candles tied in bunches should not be lit

String of gold stars wrapped around candleholder

CANDLES IN HOLDERS
*Support tall, graceful candles
in holders made from glass and
gilded wood, here decorated with
chandelier-style droplets, twinkly
gold stars, and rich satin tassels.*

FREESTANDING CANDLES
*Jazz up chunky, freestanding candles by
adding ribbons and brocade, spiraling cord
around them, or tying a gold leaf to the front.
Choose novelty candles with unusual shapes
and finishes such as glossy or marbled gold.*

Blue and gold
tassel adorns a
church candle

Gold tassel threaded
onto sparkly gold
elastic wound around
a chunky candle

Ribbon and
gold-sprayed
oak leaves adorn
a chunky cream
candle

DECORATED CANDELABRAS

TRANSFORM A SIMPLE wrought-iron candelabra into a stunning table centerpiece by winding glossy evergreen leaves around the branched arms and scattering gold foil leaves among rich red roses. Adapt the idea with more dense foliage and artificial grapes, bright satin cord, and colored candles or, for a more formal party, dangle jewel-like beads below navy beeswax candles.

Christmas tree decoration

LUSH GREENERY
Enliven a candelabra with a bounteous display made by entwining glossy evergreen leaves among the branches. Hang bunches of lustrous artificial grapes from the leaves and add pale green candles to finish.

Satin cord hides the black candelabra

Tapered candle made of rolled beeswax

MEXICAN-STYLE CANDELABRA
Wind brightly colored satin cord tightly around the branches of a black candelabra and add candles in colors to match. Glamorous Christmas tree decorations in matching colors give a festive feel.

Hanging gold stars catch the light

EVENING ELEGANCE
Thread delicate blue glass beads and festive gold stars onto fine wire and wrap them in and out of the candelabra branches. Add movement with pretty drops hanging down, and finish with unusual midnight blue candles of rolled beeswax.

FRESH FLOWERS

A fresh arrangement made by winding ivy and roses around a candelabra creates a stunning centerpiece for a special party. If the display needs to last for the whole festive season, use artificial flowers and greenery instead.

Cream candles complement the dense colors

Gold foil leaves on wire stems from cake-decorating stores

Rich red rose wired to ivy and gold foil leaves

Wiring roses

Place an ivy leaf on its stem behind a rosebud so that the two stems lie together. Push floral wire through the bottom of the rosebud and wind it down around both stems to the bottom. Holding the wired stems in one hand and florist's tape in the other, twist the stems to wind the tape around them, binding them together.

Twig Chandelier

GIVE A VINE WREATH A NEW LEASE OF LIFE by turning it into a spectacular twig chandelier complete with burning candles. Adorn it with dried fruit, chilies, gilded nuts, and seedpods, and add sparkling glass droplets to catch the light. Hang your chandelier over the dinner table for elegant festive dining or use the glass of a nearby mirror to reflect the warm glow of the candles around the room.

Twig Chandelier Ingredients

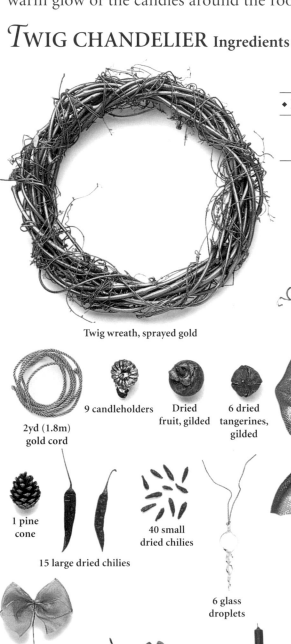

Twig wreath, sprayed gold

2yd (1.8m) gold cord

9 candleholders

Dried fruit, gilded

6 dried tangerines, gilded

1 pine cone

15 large dried chilies

40 small dried chilies

6 glass droplets

6 wired bows

10 dried tropical seedpods, gilded

4 pecans, gilded

9 Christmas tree candles

◆ EQUIPMENT ◆

Scissors

Strong glue

Dried tangerine with gilding creme rubbed onto the skin

BURNING BRIGHT
Never leave the twig chandelier burning unattended, and make sure you replace the candles as they burn down.

Tree decoration or replacement chandelier droplet from a lighting store

MAKING THE CHANDELIER

1 *Cut the cord into three lengths of 24in (60cm). Tie them to the wreath equal distances apart and knot them together at the top. Clip the candleholders around the wreath.*

2 *Use a strong glue to attach the dried fruit, tangerines, pine cone, chilies, seedpods, and pecans.*

3 *Hang the chandelier. Position the candles and glass droplets then add the wired bows to finish.*

FROSTED CENTERPIECE

DELIGHT YOUR DINNER GUESTS with this abundant table centerpiece, smothered in sparkling sugar-frosted fruit that glitters in the candlelight. Use thick creamy candles, frosted fruit, candied peel, dried flowers, and artificial berries in colors to complement the table setting. If all the fresh fruit is frosted, the centerpiece should last up to one week.

FROSTED CENTERPIECE Ingredients

◆ EQUIPMENT ◆

Knife

Craft knife

Metal ruler

40 floral wires
(medium gauge)

**Block florist's foam,
9 x 4½ x 3¼in
(22.5 x 11 x 7.5cm)**

**Silver cake board,
10 x 6½in (25 x 16cm)**

**2 candles,
6½in (16cm) high**

**1 candle,
9½in (24cm) high**

**15 sprigs
dried leaves**

**12 dried
hydrangea heads**

**10 bunches dried,
dyed broom**

17 poppy heads

**12 bunches
artificial berries**

**15 dried
pink rosebuds**

**20 dried
peach rosebuds**

**10 wired bows
(see page 68)**

**3 frosted
pears**

**4 slices candied
citron peel**

**7 small bunches
frosted grapes**

**Frosted
purple fig**

**Candied
green fig**

**2 candied
tangerines**

**Candied
greengage plum**

**6 frosted
kumquats**

**5 frosted slices
star fruit**

LIVING FLAME
*Replace candles before they
burn down to the level of the
highest piece of fruit.*

Candied fruit
does not need
frosting

Bow made with
green ribbon
(see page 68)

Rosebuds wired
into bunches

MAKING THE FROSTED CENTERPIECE

Prepare the frosted fruit in advance to allow it time to dry (see opposite), bend ribbon to make wired bows (see page 68), and twist floral wire around the stems of small bunches of berries, rosebuds, and broom to secure them in the foam.

1 Measure the diameter of the candles, cut holes for them in the cake board, and place it on the block of florist's foam. Push the tallest candle through the center hole and flank with the two shorter candles.

2 Push the sprigs of dried leaves and hydrangea heads into the florist's foam below the cake board.

3 Add the wired bunches of broom and the poppy heads between the dried leaves and hydrangeas.

Push in items at different angles to make the display look more natural

Frosting fruit

1 Wash and dry the fruit to ensure that the skin is clean. Lightly whisk the whites of two eggs in a bowl and use a pastry brush to apply it to the prepared fruit skin.

4 Fill in all the gaps by pushing the wire stems of the artificial berries and rosebuds into the florist's foam.

Individual rosebuds wired into bunches

2 Use a spoon to sprinkle finely granulated sugar gently over the fruit. This gives a more delicate, frosted look than rolling the fruit in sugar.

5 Pile the frosted fruit and candied peel on the cake board to hide it from view completely. To finish, fill any gaps with a scattering of ribbon bows, fastened by pushing the wire stems into the foliage.

3 Leave the fruit to dry on a wire rack. When frosted it will last for up to one week.

LANTERNS

A CLUSTER OF FESTIVE LANTERNS twinkling
on the porch guides guests to the front
door at Christmas. Buy lanterns ready-
made and embellish them with beads,
fancy cords, and Christmas tree
decorations, or make your own using small
glass jars and night-light candles. Use glass
paint in rich, jewel colors, add stars and
snowflakes with gold paste, or use the
sponge-painting technique on page 126.

Right, from top to bottom:
MOONLIGHT LANTERN
Spray a metal lantern with gold paint and
paint a red moon on one of the glass sides.

RED AND GREEN POT
Paint red and green stripes on a small jar hung
from a simple wire harness threaded with beads.

GREEN GARDEN LIGHT
Wrap wire around the rim of a green glass
holder, and suspend it from a spiral of wire.

Center, from top to bottom:
TREE LANTERN
Decorate a store-bought lantern with red glass
paint and hang it from a length of green cord.

FANCY LANTERN
Embellish a store-bought lantern with gold stars
painted on the glass and dangling beneath.

LARGE RED LANTERN
Hang a lustrous moon from the bottom of a red-
painted tin lantern suspended from gold cord.

Far right, from top to bottom:
GLOWING GREEN GLASS
Place a small green glass in a store-bought wire
holder decorated with luminous beads.

STARLIGHT POT
Paint colored stars, moons, and dots on a red
glass pot and hang it from a spiral of green wire.

LARGE OUTDOOR LANTERN
Paint gold stars on the glass of a dark green
lantern and add a tall cream candle.

RED CANDLEHOLDER
Hook a loose spiral of wire around a tapered
glass holder and glue beads in place on the wire.

ROCOCO MANTELPIECE

THE PLUSH VELVET on this sumptuous Christmas mantelpiece is punctuated with winter flowers in deep shades, jewel-colored glasses, and cut glass tree decorations. Smother the shelf in a piece of rich velvet with gold braid sewn along the scalloped edge. Add gilded accessories, opulent festive baubles, and a garland made with wire-edged silk ribbons.

Beeswax candle suits the matte gold wooden candlestick

Anemones, spray roses, and scarlet nerines interspersed with loops of sparkly blue ribbon

Steel holder sprayed gold and filled with florist's foam

Fresh orange wrapped with braid secured with upholstery pins

Gilded picture frame
with braided edge
and blue velvet inset

Gold tree decoration
tied with gauzy ribbon

Dried orange with carved
skin (see page 31)

Decorative gold
wire shapes catch
the light

Red velvet pelmet
decorated with
silk ribbons

SILVER MANTELPIECE

THIS WINTRY LOOK is warmed by the glow of frosted glass oil lamps and decorated with festive silver accessories that gleam in the firelight. Adorn a pelmet of painted-silver cardboard with paper doilies and variegated holly leaves, and add life with cream tulips and a tree of pale green leaves.

Painted wooden frame with corrugated inset and glass grapes

Elegant urn surrounded by a string of silver beads

Silver cardboard pelmet trimmed with holly leaves, doilies, and frosty baubles

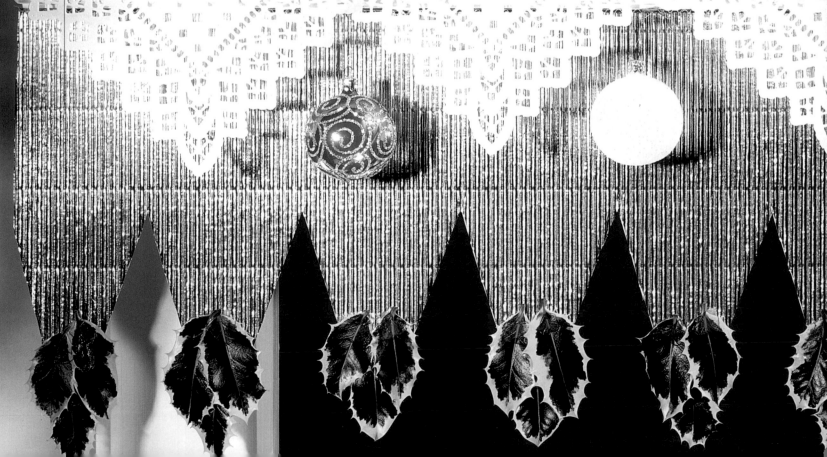

Silver-green helichrysum
sprigs and silver baubles
pushed into florist's foam

Lid of a silver
star-shaped box

Silver and pearl
baubles in an
etched glass goblet

HOMESPUN MANTELPIECE

NATURAL COLORS AND MATERIALS are central to this traditional look. Dried citrus fruit, bunches of cinnamon sticks, pressed tin birds, and festive pastry-cutters sit on top of the mantel, and a garland packed with dried fruit, nuts, and craft dough shapes (see page 20) hangs beneath.

Miniature Christmas tree decorated with tiny spice cookies

Pastry-cutters hung from ribbon

Bay leaves tacked to a foam ball

Painted wooden frame and checked fabric inset adorned with craft dough tree

Jolly star-shaped lollipops sit in a festive mug

Pressed tin heart

Plain church candle

Cones and wooden fruit fill a Christmas bowl

Tiny woven basket filled with foil-wrapped chocolate balls

SUNSHINE MANTELPIECE

A COLORFUL DISPLAY brings the warmth of the sun to the
Christmas festivities in your home. Choose real and paper
flowers in the brightest colors and keep accessories natural
in straw, pressed tin, wood, and paper. Trim
the mantel with easily made paper
bunting to create a party
mood, and echo the
citrus shades with
vibrant candles.

Coil of
gold wire
with stars

Heavy papier-mâché box
containing ranunculus,
poppies, and gold-sprayed
dried eucalyptus leaves

Paper rosettes glued
onto sticks, mixed
with gold moons
and bead flowers

Punched
tin vase

Blue wooden vase filled
with spice balls (see
page 30) and metal
fruit and vegetables

Tinplate
fish (see
page 46)

SEASONAL GIFTS, CARDS, & STATIONERY

A growing number of telltale white envelopes in the mailbox heralds the approach of Christmas, when unique handcrafted cards will be treasured by the recipient. Give gifts a special treatment, too, with stylish and witty handprinted wrapping papers, and add complementary gift tags and clever decorations to prove that details really do count.

GIFT WRAP

MAKE GIFTS FOR FRIENDS and relatives extra special by designing your own sumptuous wrapping papers to shimmer enticingly under the tree. Print festive motifs on colored paper, or brush a thick paint and paste mixture over plain paper and scrape off interesting patterns. Buy rolls of inexpensive paper to work on, or be more extravagant with colored tissue, and textured and recycled papers.

BLOCK PRINTING Ingredients

Pencil eraser

Pastry cutter

Balsa wood

Cork

Paper

◆ EQUIPMENT ◆

Craft knife

Glue

Paintbrush

Opaque waterproof paint

PASTE-GRAIN PAPER
Ingredients

Opaque waterproof paint

Thick cardboard

Wallpaper paste

Paper

◆ EQUIPMENT ◆

Shallow bowl

Spoon or spatula

Wide paintbrush

Scissors

Cardboard block-print partridge with gold nail-head eye

Pencil eraser block print and nail-head berries

Pencil eraser block print

Coiled string and wooden block print

PRINTED PAPERS
Transform plain or colored paper into eye-catching gift wrap with simple block and paste-grain prints.

Cardboard comb and wooden block print

BLOCK PRINTING

Search for wooden fabric-printing blocks to print with, or make your own from a pencil eraser. Natural sponges and coiled string can also be used to create interesting prints, or original designs can be cut from cardboard or carved into potatoes.

1 Push the pastry cutter firmly through the pencil eraser to make a leaf-shaped rubber block for the stamp.

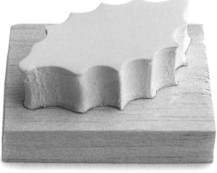

2 Cut a piece of balsa wood slightly larger than the rubber stamp and glue them together.

3 Carve extra detail, such as a vein, into the leaf. Trim the cork and glue it to the balsa wood to act as a handle.

Add details such as holly berries using knitting needles or nail heads dipped in paint

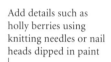

4 Brush some paint onto the stamp, avoiding the carved detail, and press onto the paper to print.

PRETTY PRINTS
Liven up plain red construction paper with colorful clusters of leaves. Add gold berries for festive extravagance.

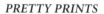

Other Ideas

Cardboard stamp
Draw a motif on a piece of cardboard and cut it out. Glue it to a larger piece of cardboard and attach a cork to the back as a handle.

String print
Coil a piece of string, press it onto some gluey paper, and cut around it. Secure a cork to the back.

Potato print
Cut a potato in half and use a small kitchen knife to cut a pattern into the cut side of one half.

Sponge print
Dip a natural sponge lightly into gold paint and dab on paper for a shimmery effect.

MAKING PASTE-GRAIN PAPER

A thick mixture of wallpaper paste and paint gives rich color and texture to plain paper. Scrape away eye-catching patterns with a comb cut from sturdy cardboard or use different household objects for a range of effects.

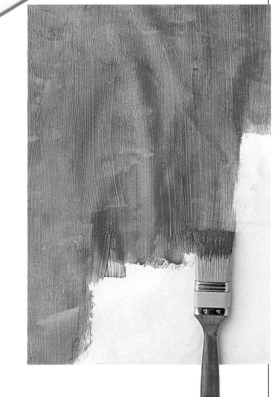

1 In a shallow bowl, mix some wallpaper paste with water according to the instructions on the package.

2 Once the paste has thickened, gradually mix paint into it until it reaches the desired color.

3 Use a wide paintbrush to coat the paper with the mixture. Brush it on roughly for a textured effect.

4 Cut thick cardboard into a comb shape and use it to scrape a swirling or zigzag pattern into the wet paint and paste mixture. Leave to dry.

Swirling pattern made with 6-tooth comb

Other Ideas

Printing block
Press a clean wooden fabric-printing block onto the wet paint and paste. Add squiggly lines using a pastry wheel.

Pastry wheel
Run a pastry wheel across wet paint and paste for wiggly lines.

Fork
Choose a fork with equal-length prongs for a simple yet stunning effect. Wash the fork carefully after use.

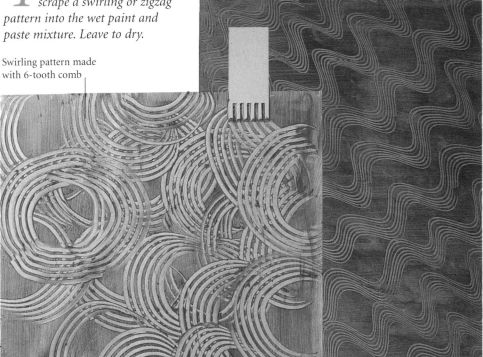

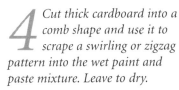

GIFT BOXES

ADD A HINT OF MYSTERY to a special gift by presenting it in a luxurious custom-made box. Choose cardboard in colors that complement the gift and hand-print it with festive designs (see pages 100-101) for an even more personal touch. Lush bows of gauzy ribbon, or rich gold cord and tassels, offer a final flourish for a truly elegant box.

MAKING A RECTANGULAR BOX

Vary the measurements given on the template above to suit the size of your gift.

RECTANGULAR BOX Ingredients

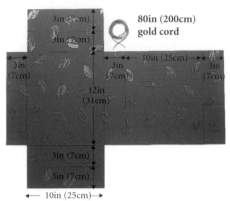

80in (200cm) gold cord

3in (7cm)
3in (7cm)
3in (7cm)
10in (25cm)
3in (7cm)
3in (7cm)
12in (31cm)
3in (7cm)
3in (7cm)
10in (25cm)

TEMPLATE
Colored cardboard,
24 x 29in (59 x 71cm)

The measurements given here make the largest of the rectangular boxes shown.

◆ EQUIPMENT ◆

Pencil

Plastic ruler

Cutting mat

Craft knife

Metal ruler

Glue (optional)

Single-hole punch

1 *Using a pencil and ruler, mark out the dimensions given on the template onto the decorated side of the cardboard.*

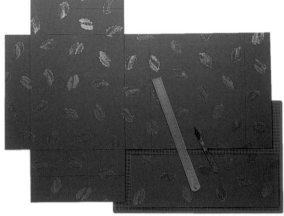

2 *Place the cardboard on a cutting mat and use a sharp craft knife and metal ruler to cut carefully around the outside edge of the template as shown.*

3 *Align the metal ruler with the remaining pencil lines and score lightly along each one.*

4 *Fold the cardboard inward along the scored lines to create a box. To close it, tie gold cord or ribbon around the box. It is not necessary to glue the box closed, but it will be more secure if you do.*

PYRAMID BOX Ingredients

18in (45cm)
ribbon

TEMPLATE
Colored cardboard,
21 x 21in
(54 x 54cm)

7in
(18cm)

7in
(18cm)

7in (18cm)

The measurements
given here make the
small pyramid in
the foreground.

PYRAMID BOX

*Mark out the template on cardboard, then
cut and score as for the rectangular box.
Using a single-hole punch, make a hole in
each of the four points. Thread a ribbon
through the holes, gently pull the points
together, and tie in a simple bow.*

FESTIVE BOXES

*Wrap gifts in layers of colored
tissue paper and tie the
boxes loosely to show a
splash of color within.*

Square box

Small
rectangular box

Tall pyramid

Large
rectangular box

Small pyramid

RIBBONS & BOWS

FINISH A BEAUTIFULLY WRAPPED package with a length of lavish ribbon tied in a generous bow. Experiment with interesting brocade, raffia, and strings of glitzy sequins, or visit stationery stores for paper ribbons in unusual colors and textures. Be creative with romantic flower bows and opulent double bows, or make it quick and easy with a simple cheat's bow. (See opposite page).

Coarse-weave
wire-edged ribbon

Shot taffeta with
gold wire edge

WIRE-EDGED RIBBONS
Use a wire-edged ribbon to make a pretty rose-shaped bow, as well as to give support to all other types of bows.

Wire-edged organza

Wire-edged striped taffeta

Twisted paper

Open weave jute

Curling ribbon

Braided flat cord

Gold-flecked tissue paper

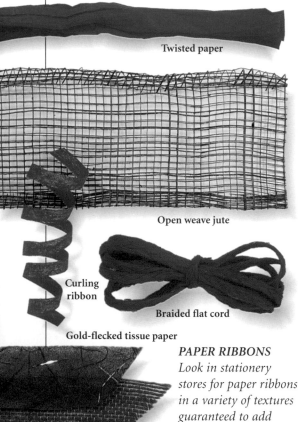

PAPER RIBBONS
Look in stationery stores for paper ribbons in a variety of textures guaranteed to add interest to gift wrapping.

Cotton webbing

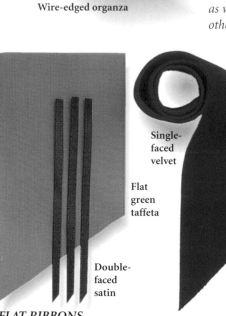

Single-faced velvet

Flat green taffeta

Double-faced satin

FLAT RIBBONS
Satin or velvet ribbons are ideal for making elegant flat bows.

Woven gold cord

Gimp edging

Single row sequins

CORDS AND SEQUINS
Try the notions department of a large sewing store for more unusual types of ribbon.

Organza with gold edging

ORGANZA RIBBONS
Wispy organza ribbons make exquisite bows for glamorous gifts.

Organza with taffeta stripes

CHEAT'S BOW Using wire-edged ribbon

1 Make a loop in the center of the ribbon and hold it where the tails cross.

2 Pull the top of the loop down behind the cross to form two small loops.

3 Wrap a long piece of wire around the middle of the bow to secure it.

Trim the ends of the ribbon as required

DOUBLE BOW Using wire-edged ribbon

1 Holding the ribbon at its center, bring half of the left tail up underneath to make a loop. Hold it in position. Repeat to make a second, slightly larger loop underneath.

2 Hold the loops in place with your left hand and repeat step 1 using the right-hand tail of ribbon to make two loops. Pinch all four loops in the center to hold.

3 Fold a short piece of the same ribbon in half lengthwise and wrap around the center of the bow. Twist a wire around the two ends at the back to secure.

Trim the ends of the ribbon diagonally

ROSE BOW Using wire-edged ribbon and beaded wire stamens

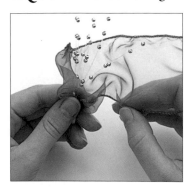

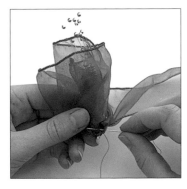

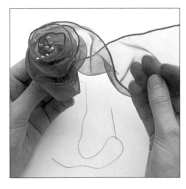

1 Hold the bottom of the wire stamens in one hand and start to wind the ribbon loosely around them in a circle, pinching the bottom.

2 After each wrap, sew a few small stitches in the bottom to hold the bow together. Continue wrapping, fanning out the top as you go.

3 Near the end of the ribbon, twist it as you wrap to create a petal effect. Tuck the end down toward the bottom and sew to secure.

Fluff out the top of the rose to make it look flowerlike

FINISHING TOUCHES

SMALL CHRISTMAS TREE DECORATIONS, artificial berries, dried fruit and flowers, shells, pieces of costume jewelry and little trinkets are all worth saving to make into original accessories for wrapped gifts. Glue or wire unusual knickknacks together to complement or boldly contrast with the style of the wrapping, then tape or hook the arrangement to a decorative ribbon and remember to add a quirky homemade gift tag (see page 110).

Gold brocade decoration acts as a mount for the tassel

NATURAL ITEMS

Pine cone

Holly leaf

Dried orange segment

Polished shells

Cinnamon sticks

Dried rosebud

ARTIFICIAL ITEMS

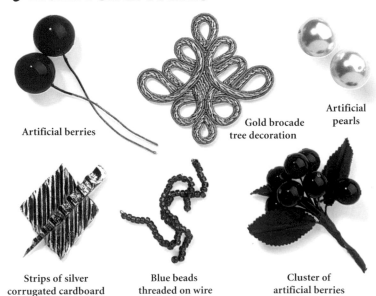

Artificial berries

Gold brocade tree decoration

Artificial pearls

Strips of silver corrugated cardboard

Blue beads threaded on wire

Cluster of artificial berries

GOLD AND GLITZY
Create this opulent festive accessory by gluing together two store-bought Christmas tree decorations.

Luxurious gold tassel shimmers in the light

Slices of orange dried on a flat surface

FRUIT CLUSTER
Three slices of dried orange glued together look attractive topped with cheat's bows in copper-colored satin and organza ribbon (see previous page).

White paper flowers
sprayed gold

Gold stamens
from a cake
decorating store

Dark green
mesh ribbon
enhances the
outdoor theme

GILDED POSY
*Twist the stems of gold paper flowers and
stamens together with loops of gold ribbon. Add
a touch of color with blue beads threaded on wire,
and bind all the stems with gold cord to secure.*

Silver cord
loops

TRADITIONAL HOLLY
*Tie cinnamon sticks together with a bow
made from open-weave ribbon, then attach
with wire to stems of holly. Dried rosebuds
secured with gold thread and wired to the
front of the bow add a decorative detail.*

SEASHELLS AND PEARLS
*Glue shells, pearls, and a bunch of
lustrous artificial grapes to an oval of silver
corrugated cardboard, and top with flat silver
cord gathered into loops.*

Store-bought
artificial berries

Bound stems of
paper rose and
artificial berries

FESTIVE BERRIES
*Bind the stems of bunches
of artificial berries to a red
paper rose and glue a red
cheat's bow (see page 105)
and a pine cone to the front.*

BRONZE BOW
*Loop a wire-edged organza ribbon to make
a rosette and secure with wire at the back.
A cedar cone glued to the center provides a
contrast in texture.*

LUXURY WRAPPINGS

STEAL THE LIMELIGHT under the Christmas tree with imaginatively wrapped gifts that make use of the wide range of unusual papers available in craft stores. Mix and match colors, textures, and fabrics, and add panache with silk and satin ribbons, exotic feathers, glittery stars, and shiny baubles. For a stylish, natural look try brown paper, dried seed pods, and pressed leaves, or contrast a glitzy wrapping and a single leaf for maximum impact.

WHITE BOX Ingredients

Lengths of white and gold paper pleated into fans

5 small baubles on wires

Glossy gold cord

Gold and white wrapping paper

Strips of pleated white paper

OTHER IDEAS

THE NATURAL LOOK
Glue a random pattern of dried leaves to textured brown paper. Tie with braided raffia, adding loose strands tied in a bow on top. Finish the look with an exotic dried fruit.

A TOUCH OF GLAMOUR
Tie red foil crepe paper with a wide orange taffeta ribbon and top it with a red rose bow made from silk ribbon (see page 105). A dried leaf contrasts with the elegant swirls of the chiffon ribbon tucked beneath the bow.

SHIMMERING STARS
Cover dark purple crepe paper with glassine paper to give a glossy effect. Tie a lush satin ribbon in a bow and add silver rickrack braid. Mount a glittery star on wire and attach it to the ribbon to twinkle enticingly.

MAGIC AND MYSTERY
Gather a large rectangle of stiff fabric such as dupion silk around the gift and tie with a contrasting silk ribbon. Hint at festive decadence by tucking two exotic feathers under the ribbon.

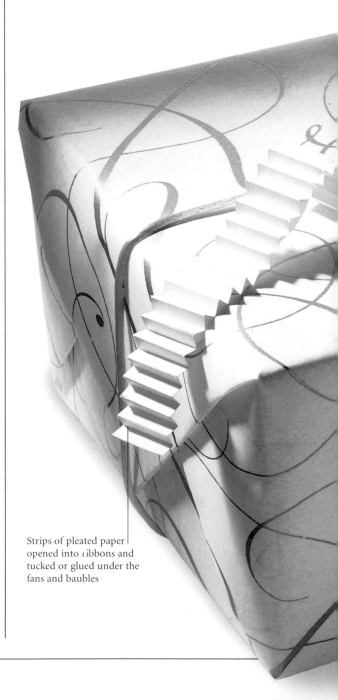

Strips of pleated paper opened into ribbons and tucked or glued under the fans and baubles

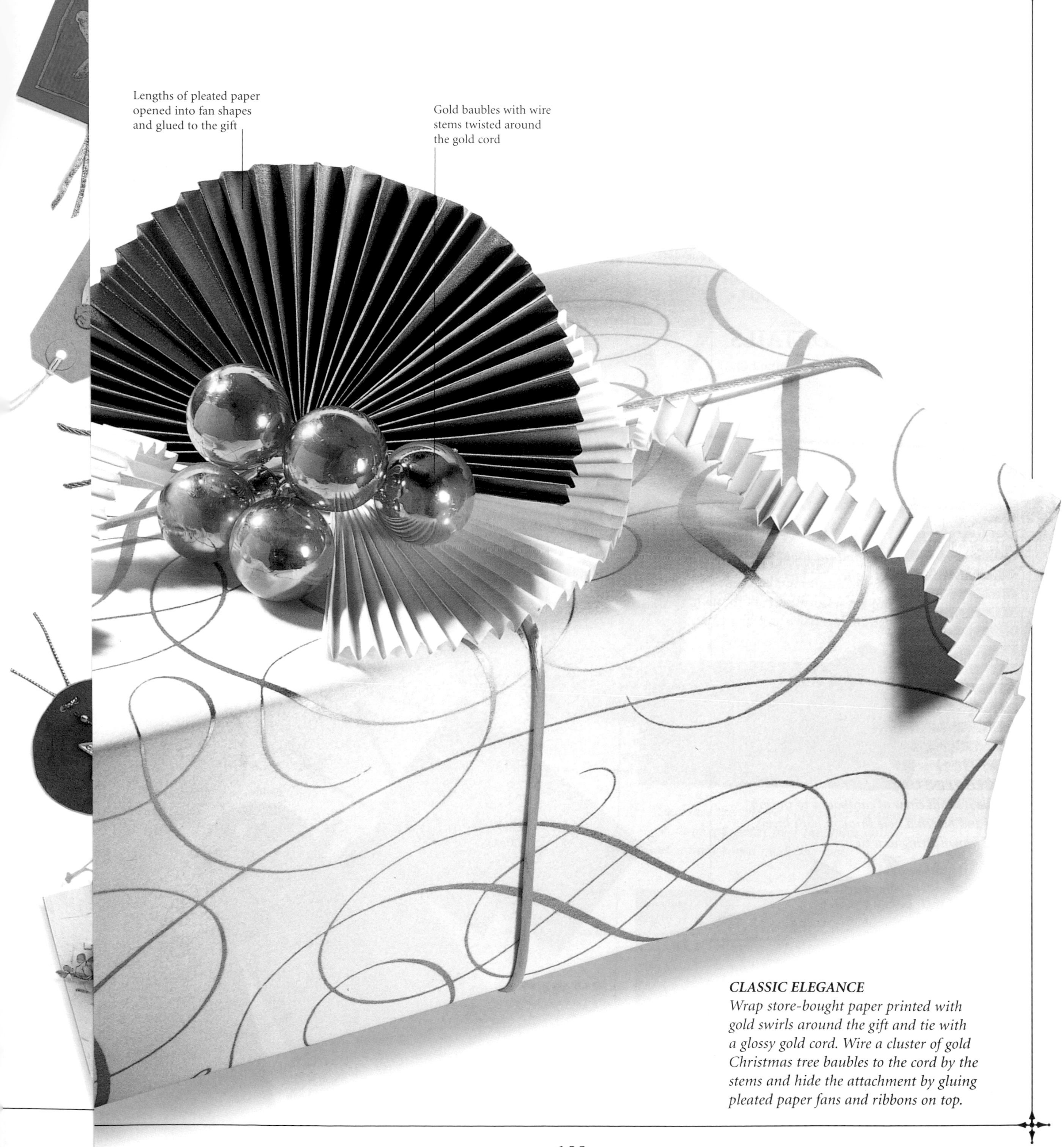

Lengths of pleated paper
opened into fan shapes
and glued to the gift

Gold baubles with wire
stems twisted around
the gold cord

CLASSIC ELEGANCE
*Wrap store-bought paper printed with
gold swirls around the gift and tie with
a glossy gold cord. Wire a cluster of gold
Christmas tree baubles to the cord by the
stems and hide the attachment by gluing
pleated paper fans and ribbons on top.*

CHRISTMAS CARDS

THE BEAUTY OF THESE EYE-CATCHING Christmas cards lies in their simplicity. Start collecting interesting papers and cards, pretty pieces of ribbon and braid, tiny beads from unwanted necklaces and shiny gold decorations, and use them to create unique cards for friends and family.

COLLAGE CARD
Decorate festive red construction paper with torn squares of rough-textured paper. Create depth by gathering a piece of gold wire-edged ribbon into a flower shape and gluing it on top.

Gummed foil cupids
from stationery stores

SWIRLS AND CUPIDS
Cut a piece of hand-decorated paper (see page 101) and glue it to textured cardboard in a contrasting color. Finish with gold-foil cupids in a random pattern.

KNOT AND BRAID CARD
Glue a snippet of heavy metallic braid and a knot of gold cord to textured red cardboard. A small piece of metal ribbon glued across the top of the braid prevents fraying.

BIJOU BOWS
Loop gold brocade into a bow and attach to turquoise cardboard. For added interest tuck a gold leaf beneath the bow (see center card).

Gold beads secured with glue

RECYCLED LOOK
Juxtapose torn recycled paper with luxurious cream cardboard and cover with a scattering of small gold beads.

CARDBOARD AND CORD
Glue recycled cream paper to finely corrugated brown cardboard and add a loop of gold cord. Sketch a design in pencil and accentuate it with small beads glued over the top.

Beads glued in place over a design sketched in pencil

TEXTURED PAPER
Beautifully textured handmade paper hardly needs extra embellishment. Simply add a brown corrugated cardboard leaf to continue the natural theme.

PAPYRUS EFFECT
Glue layers of papyrus to cream ribbed cardboard. Cut two slots in the center, pass the wires of a gold foil leaf through both slots, and tape at the back to secure.

PATTERNED LEAF
Cut a leaf shape from hand-decorated paper (see page 101) and attach it diagonally across a piece of construction paper in contrasting festive red.

NOVELTY CARDS

DELIGHTFUL NOVELTY CARDS, like this bejeweled festive tree and woolly sheep with its beady eye, are remarkably easy to make using the templates on pages 187–88. Let your imagination run riot with alternative designs, and experiment with exciting materials to create highly original cards that will delight the children and be proudly displayed on the mantelpiece at Christmas.

NOVELTY CARDS Ingredients

Thin green wire

Cream curling ribbon

Brown curling ribbon

Green cardboard, plain cardboard, and textured paper

Small beads

◆ EQUIPMENT ◆

Pencil

Craft knife

Cutting mat

Metal ruler

Scissors

Glue

MAKING THE TREE Using the template on page 187

1 Copy the template onto green cardboard and cut it out with a craft knife.

2 Turn the cardboard over and score vertically down the center. Fold it in half.

3 Cut three wires, each long enough to join both sides of the card. Thread tiny beads onto the wire, twisting a small loop after every few.

4 Make three tiny holes in each side of the tree (see inset). Push the ends of the wire through to the back and twist a loop at each end to secure.

MAKING THE SHEEP Using the template on page 188

1 Copy the template onto plain cardboard and cut it out. Score across the center fold.

2 Cut out the sheep's coat from textured paper and glue it on. Fold the sheep inward along the score line so it can stand.

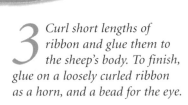

3 Curl short lengths of ribbon and glue them to the sheep's body. To finish, glue on a loosely curled ribbon as a horn, and a bead for the eye.

AUTHENTIC TOUCHES
Delight children with a sheep that really rocks and a Christmas tree with jewel-like beads strung between the branches.

Twists in the wire separate the beads and allow movement

Fleecy coat made from curled ribbon

Curved base acts as a rocker

MENUS & INVITATIONS

CREATE PERSONAL INVITATIONS and menu cards using thin cardboard embellished with rich satin cords or silvery ribbons woven in and out of slits and tied in bows. Enliven simple designs with quirky details such as tiny square holes or fancy silver stitching and use the same techniques to make place cards for a dinner party.

MENU CARD Ingredients

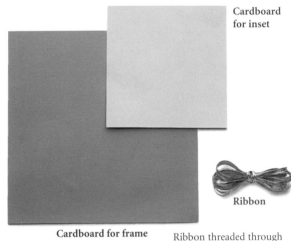

Cardboard for inset

Cardboard for frame

Ribbon

◆ EQUIPMENT ◆

Ruler

Scissors

Pencil

Craft knife

Metal ruler

Cutting mat

Masking tape

Sewing on cardboard

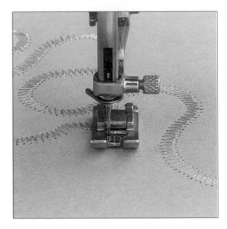

Cut the cardboard to the size required, then thread the sewing machine with metallic silver thread and select zigzag stitch. As you sew, carefully move the cardboard around, like a piece of fabric, to produce decorative swirls of silver stitching.

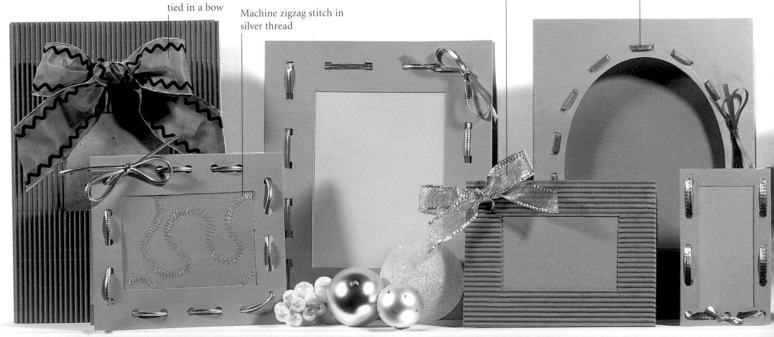

Ribbon threaded through two slits in the frame and tied in a bow

Machine zigzag stitch in silver thread

Silver voile ribbon threaded through two slits in a corrugated frame

Store-bought frame decorated with ribbon threaded through slits

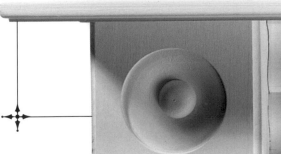

MAKING THE MENU CARD

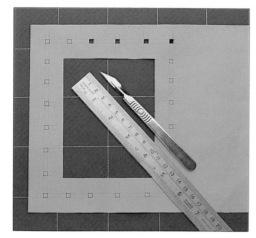

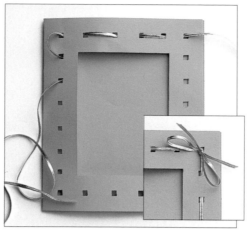

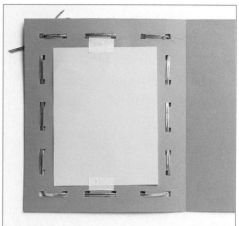

1 Cut out a suitable-sized rectangle of cardboard and fold in half. Open it out and draw the frame in pencil on the front. Draw tiny squares around it and cut them out with a craft knife and metal ruler.

2 Starting at the top right-hand corner, thread the ribbon in and out of the square slots around the edge of the frame. When you reach the top again, tie both ends of the ribbon in a bow (see inset).

3 Write the menu on different colored cardboard and cut it out. Tape it in position behind the frame using two small pieces of masking tape so it can be removed and replaced if reusing the frame.

SHORT CUTS

If time is short, buy cardboard mats from stationery stores, glue on gift wrap to decorate and use a hole punch instead of a craft knife to make tiny holes for ribbons.

Wrapping paper glued to thin cardboard with velvet ribbon threaded down one side

Silver braid threaded through slots cut with a craft knife

Handmade paper with a rough texture

Checked voile ribbon in a store-bought frame

Silver zigzag stitch frame

Satin cord wound around the edges of the frame

STOCKINGS

A GLIMPSE OF A TEMPTING PRESENT peeking from the top of a brightly colored homemade Christmas stocking is enough to make any child's heart race with anticipation on Christmas morning. Sew or glue buttons, ribbons, felt shapes, and strings of beads to the cuffs for festive decoration and trim the edges with pinking shears for added interest.

STAR STOCKING Ingredients

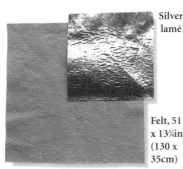

Silver lamé

Matching thread

Felt, 51 x 13¾in (130 x 35cm)

Beads

♦ EQUIPMENT ♦

Rough paper

Pencil

Scissors

Pins

Sewing machine or needle and thread

Pinking shears

Iron-on backing

Fabric glue

MAKING THE STAR STOCKING

TEMPLATE

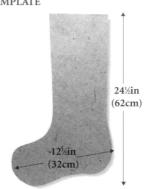

24½in (62cm)

12½in (32cm)

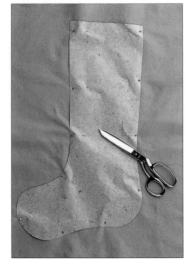

1 Copy the template onto brown paper and cut it out. Fold the felt in half and pin the template to it. Cut around the template through the double layer of felt.

RIBBONS AND ROPES
Use tiny stitches to secure wide checked ribbon, paper rope, and a narrow silver ribbon around the cuff of the stocking.

LOVE HEART
Cut a simple heart from bright pink felt and use fabric glue to secure it to a contrasting green miniature stocking.

GLOWING STARS
Glue shiny silver stars to sea green felt and add pearl beads to the center of each star.

MINI-BOWS
Sew bows of flat silver ribbon to the stocking top and glue tiny pearls to the center of each.

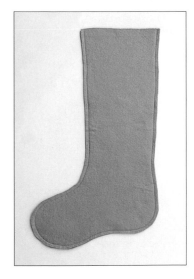

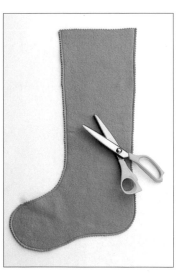

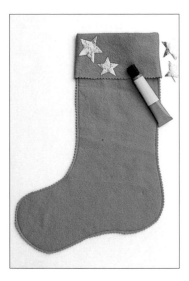

2 Sew the two felt stockings together around the edges, leaving the top open.

3 Cut around all the edges, including the top, with pinking shears.

4 Turn the top of the stocking inside out to make a cuff. Cut stars from silver lamé and glue them to the cuff. If the lamé frays, iron on a backing first.

5 Cut a small strip from the leftover felt and fold it in half. Sew it to the inside of the stocking cuff to make a secure loop for hanging.

SNOWY DROPS
Sew a string of tiny pearl beads along the top edge of the stocking, and glue or sew larger pearl beads and crystal drops randomly on the cuff.

BUTTONS
Attach a selection of pearl and glass buttons to the felt. Pack them closely for a richer look.

CLASSIC PEARLS
Cut a necklace of tiny pearly beads to size and stitch it around the cuff of a smaller stocking.

FESTIVE FELT TREES
Attach felt trees and pots to the stocking with glue. Decorate with tiny beads.

SILVER RIBBON
Glue two bands of flat silver ribbon around the top of the stocking for quick and easy style.

GIFT-FILLED ADVENT CALENDAR

THIS ENCHANTING FABRIC Advent calendar consists of 24 small pockets, each decorated with a checked appliqué shape or number (see templates on pages 186–87). Stuff the pockets with little wooden toys, foil-wrapped candies, gingerbread shapes, miniature crackers, and gold-painted nuts, which are sure to delight a child in the days just before Christmas.

Ingredients

Scraps of fabric

Felt, 42½ x 18in (106 x 45cm)
Backing material, 60 x 18in (150 x 45cm)

Beads

Ribbon

32½in (82cm) cord

2 x 4in (10cm) strips fringing

22in (57cm) wooden dowel

◆ EQUIPMENT ◆

Ruler

Scissors

Iron

Pen

Sewing machine

Needle and thread

Fabric glue

Pins

24 gifts

MAKING THE ADVENT CALENDAR

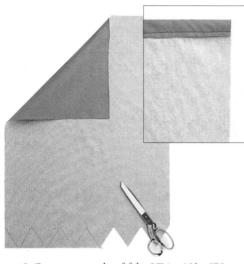

1 Cut a rectangle of felt, 27½ x 18in (70 x 45cm). Iron on the backing material. Mark and cut a zigzag pattern across the bottom. Fold the top 1¼in (3cm) over and sew it in place to make a tube (see inset).

2 Cut four strips of felt, each 3¾ x 18in (9 x 45cm). Pin them across the rectangle, equal distances apart, then sew along the bottom and up the sides of each strip, leaving the tops open.

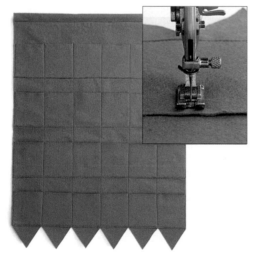

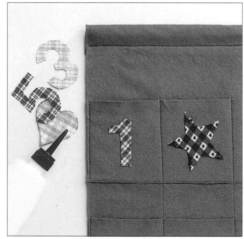

3 Divide the horizontal strips into six equal-sized pouches for the gifts by sewing a vertical line from the bottom of the bottom strip to the top of the top strip every 3in (7.5cm) across.

4 Iron backing material onto the appliqué fabric and cut out numbers between 1 and 24 and small festive shapes. Decorate the pockets by gluing on a shape or number, and ribbons, bows, or beads.

5 Roll the fringing into two tassels and sew to the ends of the cord. Thread the dowel through the top of the calendar and tie the cord to each end. Finish, if desired, by sewing padded shapes along the bottom.

FESTIVE FABRICS
Choose muted sea green felt and simple ginghams for an understated country feel.

Tiny bows made from ribbon

Embellish the bottom of the calendar, if you wish, with fabric shapes stuffed with cotton

THE DINING TABLE

*Boisterous parties, extravagant feasts, or quiet
suppers with friends and family focus the season's
celebrations in a very special way. Usually there
is at least one important meal that demands
a beautifully presented table. Either work
around the table settings you own, or choose
a festive theme as a starting point. Then create
a feast for the eyes with an exquisite candle
centerpiece, decorated crockery, patterned table
linen, and stunning homemade accessories.*

BAROQUE TABLE SETTING

RICH, OPULENT, AND WARM, in tones of claret and gold, this table setting is ideal for a sophisticated Christmas meal. A thick brocade cloth, silk napkins, and antique bone-handled cutlery are complemented by simple glass dishes and goblets decorated with gold paint. A festive arrangement of lilies and evergreen leaves presides over the table, and clusters of winter berries in gold-painted terra-cotta pots add the finishing touch.

DECORATED GLASS BOWL Ingredients

Sponge

Glass bowl

◆ EQUIPMENT ◆

Mineral spirits

Soft cloth

Paint brush

Scissors

Dish for paint

Red glass paint

Gold glass paint

GOLD FILIGREE GOBLET Ingredients

Gold outlining paint

Goblet

Sponge

Gold glass paint

◆ EQUIPMENT ◆

Mineral spirits

Soft cloth

Dish for paint

Scissors

ADDITIONAL LUXURIES
Fill brass bowls with chocolates and almonds wrapped in gold foil, and place thick cream candles in wooden candleholders painted matte gold. Tie napkins with strings of gold beads.

DECORATING THE GLASS BOWL

Glass paints in rich jewel colors such as red and gold are ideal for decorating glassware at Christmas. If you intend to use the decorated items, choose durable nontoxic paints and avoid painting areas that will come into contact with food.

A fine-tipped paint brush gives precision when painting tiny areas

1 Prepare the glass surface for painting by cleaning it carefully with mineral spirits on a soft cloth.

2 Use a fine paint brush to apply red glass paint to the underside of the pattern on the rim of the bowl. Take care not to smudge the paint onto the bowl itself, but if you do, wipe it off quickly.

Use a large sponge cut down: the tiny holes in a small sponge give too dense a pattern

Dab the paint gently onto the glass

3 Pour a small amount of gold paint into a shallow dish or saucer. Cut a small piece of sponge.

4 Dip the sponge into a little paint and press it randomly onto the underside of the bowl. Leave to dry.

DECORATING THE GOBLET

The swirly gold pattern on this goblet is reminiscent of traditional gold filigree work. Achieve the effect by applying outlining paint straight from the tube to the outside of the goblet and the rim of a plate.

1 Prepare the glass surface for painting by cleaning it carefully with mineral spirits on a soft cloth.

2 Draw random swirls on the goblet with outlining paint. Squeeze the tube carefully to prevent blobs.

3 Draw lines on the base of the glass to create a filigree-style pattern, taking care not to make smudges.

4 Use a sponge to decorate the stem of the glass with gold paint, following the instructions for step 4 opposite.

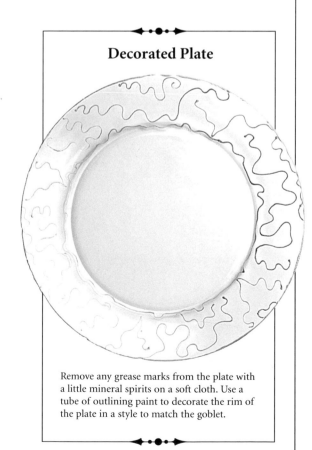

Decorated Plate

Remove any grease marks from the plate with a little mineral spirits on a soft cloth. Use a tube of outlining paint to decorate the rim of the plate in a style to match the goblet.

NATURAL TABLE SETTING

THE NATURAL MATERIALS AND EARTHY TONES of this fresh and stylish look lend themselves to a festive lunch. Dress the table up with gleaming brass and white china plates, lustrous gold glasses and wooden-handled cutlery, and echo the use of store-bought preserved and gold-sprayed oak leaves by adding a gold leaf motif to the linen tablecloth and napkins.

PRINTED TABLECLOTH Ingredients

Paper

Leaf

Tablecloth

◆ EQUIPMENT ◆

Pencil

Scissors

Kitchen knife

Paint brush

Towel

Potato

Gold fabric paint

GOLD LEAF NAPKINS Ingredients

Leaf

Paper

Gold cord

Napkin

◆ EQUIPMENT ◆

Pencil

Scissors

Pen

Needle and gold thread

Embroidery scissors

NATURAL BEAUTY

Adorn the table with a simple wreath of leaves and twigs, an ornamental cabbage, and napkins tied with brown string, gold thread, and oak leaves. Present each guest with a small gold trinket box decorated with a golden oak leaf.

FIESTA TABLE SETTING

THE VIBRANT COLORS of this table setting are perfect for a jubilant Christmas party. An array of plates and dishes in the brightest colors adorns a woven silk tablecloth with multicolored stripes, and shimmering organza napkins, frosted glassware, and translucent yellow-handled cutlery contrast with the dense colors of the scalloped chinaware and papier-mâché plates and bowls.

PAPER PLATE Ingredients

5 sheets colored tissue paper

Small paper plate

Wallpaper paste

Nontoxic water-based varnish

◆ EQUIPMENT ◆

Mixing bowl
Spoon for mixing
Wide paint brush
Medium paint brush

PAPIER-MACHE BOWL Ingredients

◆ EQUIPMENT ◆

Mixing bowl
Plastic wrap
Spoon for mixing
Scissors
Wide paint brush
Medium paint brush

China bowl

White paper

10 sheets colored tissue paper

Wallpaper paste

Nontoxic water-based varnish

EDIBLE CENTERPIECES
Arrange brightly colored chilies, squashes, kumquats, and limes in jazzy bowls and dishes.

MODERN TABLE SETTING

A CRISP, MODERN LOOK USING STARS, silver, and delicate pastels is ideal for New Year's Eve. A pale lemon brushed cotton tablecloth provides a neutral background for lustrous checked silk napkins, star-shaped napkin rings, pale earthenware, silver-sided glasses, and gleaming cutlery. Hot pink flowers with silver star collars that match the astral coasters bring a shock of warmth to the cool feel of the table.

CANDLE CENTERPIECE Ingredients

 Paper

Candles, 1½in (3.5cm) wide and 2in (5cm) high

Silver corrugated cardboard
16½ x 9in (42 x 23cm)

◆ EQUIPMENT ◆

Ruler

Pencil

Scissors

Strong glue

Matches

FLOWER COLLAR Ingredients

◆ EQUIPMENT ◆

Pencil

Ruler

Craft knife

Metal ruler

Silver corrugated cardboard

Flower   Glass and water

REFLECTING LIGHT
Add more sparkle with foil-wrapped almonds in frosted glass dishes and a candle centerpiece made with corrugated silver cardboard.

TARTAN TABLE SETTING

THE TRADITIONAL TARTAN look in holly green and berry red makes a classic evening setting for a Christmas Day or New Year's Eve feast. Soft chenille cloth, leaf green plates in textured wood and smooth china, green-handled cutlery, linen napkins, and chunky glass goblets are bathed in a rosy glow from two red candles, while homemade tartan crackers sit enticingly at each place setting.

FESTIVE CRACKERS Ingredients

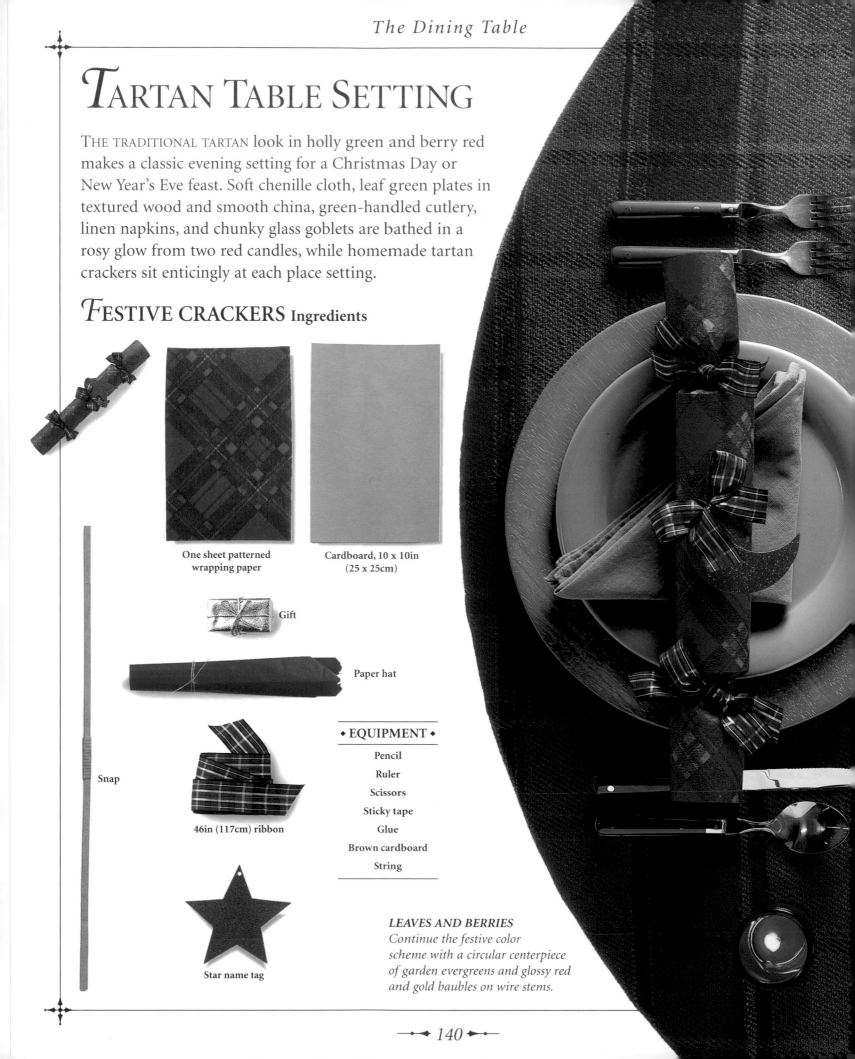

One sheet patterned wrapping paper

Cardboard, 10 x 10in (25 x 25cm)

Gift

Paper hat

Snap

46in (117cm) ribbon

Star name tag

◆ EQUIPMENT ◆

Pencil

Ruler

Scissors

Sticky tape

Glue

Brown cardboard

String

LEAVES AND BERRIES
Continue the festive color scheme with a circular centerpiece of garden evergreens and glossy red and gold baubles on wire stems.

MAKING THE CRACKER

Large and luxurious homemade Christmas crackers in a festive tartan print are extra-special when filled with carefully chosen gifts. Select a strong wrapping paper that will hold its shape when gathered at the ends of the cracker.

1 Draw a rectangle, 18 x 9¼in (45 x 23.5cm), on the wrapping paper and cut it out.

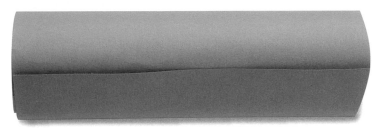

2 Cut a square, 8 x 8in (20 x 20cm), out of the cardboard and roll it into a tube, securing with tape.

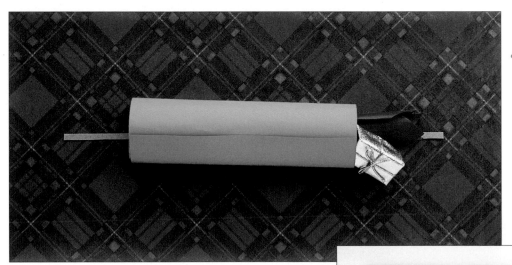

3 Place the wrapping paper face down and lay the tube in the middle. Put the snap, gift, and hat inside the tube.

4 Form the cracker by rolling the wrapping paper around the tube, then tape or glue to secure.

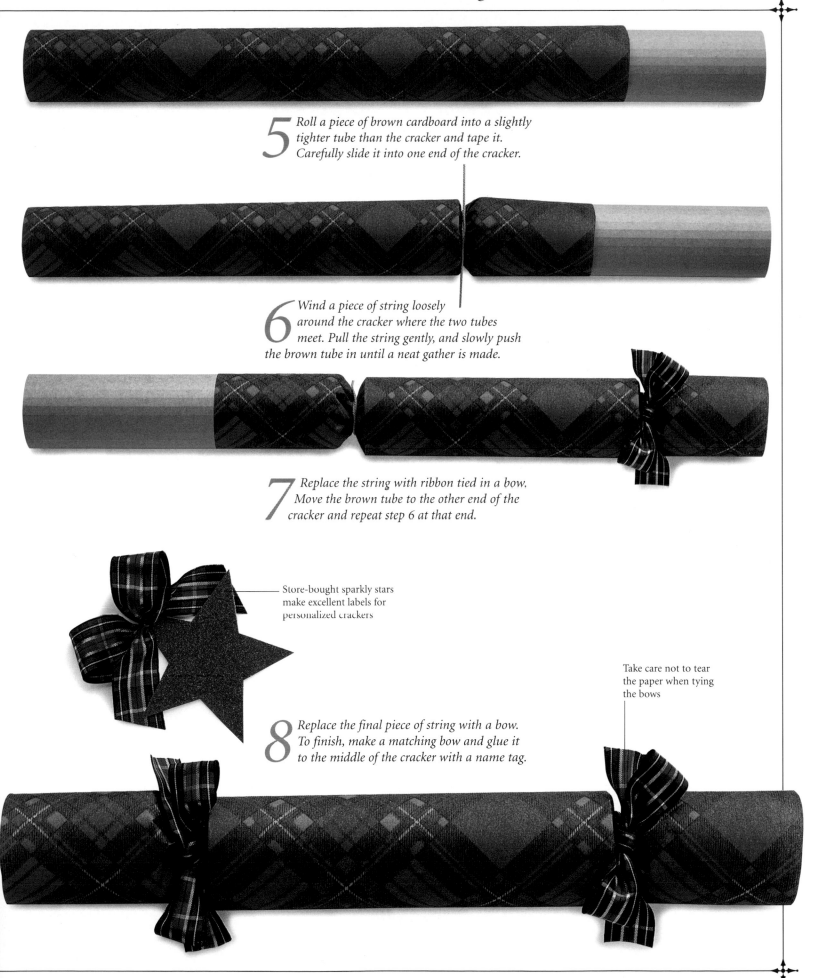

5 Roll a piece of brown cardboard into a slightly tighter tube than the cracker and tape it. Carefully slide it into one end of the cracker.

6 Wind a piece of string loosely around the cracker where the two tubes meet. Pull the string gently, and slowly push the brown tube in until a neat gather is made.

7 Replace the string with ribbon tied in a bow. Move the brown tube to the other end of the cracker and repeat step 6 at that end.

Store-bought sparkly stars make excellent labels for personalized crackers

Take care not to tear the paper when tying the bows

8 Replace the final piece of string with a bow. To finish, make a matching bow and glue it to the middle of the cracker with a name tag.

CHRISTMAS FOOD

*Christmas would not be the same without
a celebration meal, complete with traditional
decorated cakes and cookies, but why not sample
the specialties of another country for a change?
Try elegant French oyster tarts as a starter;
roast goose or venison instead of turkey;
and strudel or pavlova for a memorable
Christmas dessert. Non-meateaters can enjoy
splendid dishes of salmon, trout, and carp, while
vegetarians will be impressed with a spectacular
delicacy stuffed with wild mushrooms.*

STARTERS

BEGIN THE FESTIVE MEAL WITH A STARTER that balances and contrasts with the main dish to come. Choose from warming, hearty soups served with noodles or dumplings, delicate salads of smoked ham or marinated salmon, stylish oyster tarts or smoked salmon parcels. If you are short of time, nothing could be easier than a colorful plate of prosciutto with figs and melon or spicy boudin blanc pâté, prepared in advance: either will give an elegant, exotic feel to your Christmas dinner.

◆ BOUDIN BLANC PATE ◆

INGREDIENTS
butter, for greasing
¾ lb (375g) pork belly, chopped
½ lb (250g) chicken breast, chopped
2 onions, chopped
2 garlic cloves
4 slices (60g) fresh white bread
4 tbsp white wine
2 eggs
⅔ cup (150ml) light cream
salt and black pepper
1 tsp ground mace
4 crisp red apples
2 tbsp lemon juice
ground allspice
red pepper strips and watercress sprigs, to garnish

ILLUSTRATED BELOW
BOUDIN BLANC IS THE FRENCH VERSION OF WHITE SAUSAGE. IT IS MADE WITH WHITE MEAT SUCH AS PORK AND CHICKEN, WELL FLAVORED WITH GARLIC AND SPICES, THEN SHAPED INTO A SAUSAGE OR COOKED AS INDIVIDUAL PATES.

SERVES 6

1 Preheat the oven to 350°F/180°C. Lightly butter 6 individual ramekin dishes.

2 Place the pork, chicken breast, onion, garlic, and bread in a food processor. Blend until smooth. Add the wine, eggs, cream, salt, pepper, and mace. Blend again until the mixture is smooth.

3 Fill the ramekins with the mixture and smooth the tops. Cover the tops with foil and set the ramekins in a roasting pan. Pour in enough boiling water to come two thirds of the way up the sides of the dishes.

4 Bake the pâtés for 50–60 minutes, until firm to the touch. Remove the dishes from the pan, discard the foil, and let cool.

5 Meanwhile, core and thinly slice the apples. Sprinkle with lemon juice and allspice, place on a baking sheet lined with foil, and bake for 20 minutes. Cool.

6 Turn out the pâtés onto individual plates and garnish with thin strips of red pepper and sprigs of watercress. Serve with the apple slices and toast.

Smoked salmon parcels
(see page 148)

Boudin blanc pâté

Gravlax Salad

INGREDIENTS

2 tbsp sea salt

1 tbsp sugar

2 tsp coarsely ground black pepper

½ cup (30g) finely chopped fresh dill

2lb (1kg) salmon fillets

cooked beets, mâche, and fresh dill sprigs

MUSTARD SAUCE

2 tbsp Dijon mustard

1 tbsp white wine vinegar

1 tbsp sugar

¼ cup (60ml) olive oil

1 tbsp chopped fresh dill

ILLUSTRATED ON PAGE 172
THIS NORWEGIAN SPECIALTY HAS A
DELICATE, PEPPERY FLAVOR.

SERVES 6

1 Mix the salt, sugar, and pepper in a bowl. Sprinkle a layer of the mixture over the bottom of a shallow glass dish. Sprinkle on some of the chopped dill and lay one salmon fillet on top, skin side down.

2 Sprinkle the fillet with more salt mixture and dill, then cover with a second fillet, skin side up, arranging them head to tail.

3 Repeat with the remaining fillets, ensuring they are layered skin next to skin and flesh next to flesh. Cover the dish with plastic wrap, place a board or plate on top, and weigh down with a few weights. Leave for 2–3 hours at room temperature, then refrigerate for 3–4 days, turning the fillets daily.

4 To make the mustard sauce, whisk the ingredients in a bowl until well blended.

5 Drain the salmon fillets, thinly slice, and arrange on a serving dish with strips of beets, mâche, and dill sprigs. Serve with the mustard sauce.

Prosciutto with Figs & Melon

INGREDIENTS

1 small honeydew melon

6 fresh figs, quartered

6 slices prosciutto, cut into thin strips

fresh mint sprigs and lime slices, to garnish

DRESSING

¼ cup melon juice

¼ cup olive oil

2 tsp freshly squeezed lime juice

1 tsp clear honey

1 tsp herb mustard

salt and black pepper

ILLUSTRATED BELOW
PROSCIUTTO, ALSO KNOWN AS PARMA HAM, IS
A TRADITIONAL ITALIAN HAM THAT HAS BEEN
DRY CURED AND MATURED FOR ONE YEAR.
SLICED VERY THIN AND SERVED WITH FRESH
FIGS AND SWEET MELON, IT MAKES A LIGHT,
FESTIVE STARTER THAT IS VERY QUICK
AND EASY TO PUT TOGETHER.

SERVES 6

1 Halve the melon and scoop out the seeds. Remove the flesh with a melon baller, reserving the juices.

2 Arrange the melon balls, fig quarters, and strips of prosciutto on individual plates.

3 Whisk the melon juice, oil, lime juice, honey, mustard, salt, and pepper until well blended. Pour the dressing over each serving. Garnish with mint sprigs and a lime slice.

Christmas Eve soup
(see page 149)

**Tomato & red
pepper soup**
(see page 149)

**Prosciutto with
figs & melon**

Smoked Salmon Parcels

INGREDIENTS

8 slices smoked salmon
7oz (200g) cream cheese
2 hard-boiled eggs, chopped
1 tsp herb mustard
salt and black pepper
6 sun-dried tomatoes, drained and chopped
2 tbsp chopped fresh chives
fresh chive stems, lettuce leaves, and
lemon wedges, to garnish

ILLUSTRATED ON PAGE 146
SCOTLAND HAS ALWAYS PRODUCED SALMON WITH A SUPERIOR FLAVOR. TRY THESE DELICIOUS SMOKED SALMON PARCELS AS AN ELEGANT AND UNUSUAL STARTER.

MAKES 8

1 Trim each of the smoked salmon slices into 8 neat squares. Finely chop the remaining salmon trimmings.

2 Place the cheese, eggs, mustard, salt, and pepper in a bowl and beat until smooth. Stir in the tomatoes, chopped chives, and chopped salmon until evenly blended.

3 Place some filling in the center of each salmon square and fold the salmon over the filling to make a neat parcel.

4 Tie chive stems around each parcel to secure and place on a plate garnished with lettuce leaves and lemon wedges.

Festive Oyster Tarts

INGREDIENTS

1 cup (125g) all-purpose flour, plus extra
for kneading
salt and black pepper
6 tbsp (90g) butter, cut into small pieces
1 egg yolk
12 oysters, well scrubbed
1 tbsp olive oil
2 shallots, finely chopped
1 garlic clove, crushed
1 tbsp chopped fresh dill
1 tbsp chopped fresh tarragon
1 egg
⅔ cup (150ml) light cream
black pepper
lettuce leaves and fresh tarragon, to garnish

ILLUSTRATED ON PAGE 152
OYSTERS ARE A TYPICAL STARTER TO A FRENCH CHRISTMAS LUNCH OR DINNER.

MAKES 12

1 To make the pastry, sift the flour, salt, and pepper into a bowl. Add the butter and rub with the fingertips until fine. Mix in the egg yolk with a fork to form a firm dough, adding a little cold water if necessary. Knead on a lightly floured surface until smooth.

2 Roll out the pastry until thin and use to line 12 fluted tart pans measuring 3in (7cm). Trim off the excess pastry and press the pastry into the pans. Chill for 30 minutes. Preheat the oven to 400°F/200°C.

3 Bake the pastry shells for 5–10 minutes, until the pastry is lightly browned at the edges. Reduce the oven temperature to 375°F/190°C.

4 Open the oysters using an oyster knife. Place the oysters and their juices in a bowl.

5 Heat the oil in a skillet and cook the shallots, garlic, dill, and tarragon for 1–2 minutes, until tender. Add the oysters, reserving the juices, and cook for 1 minute.

6 Divide the mixture among the pastry cases. Beat the oyster juices with the egg, cream, and pepper and add to the pastry cases. Return to the oven for 10–15 minutes, until the filling has set. Serve garnished with lettuce leaves and fresh tarragon.

Beef Soup with Noodles

INGREDIENTS

2 tbsp vegetable oil
2lb (1kg) small beef bones
1lb (500g) shin of beef
2 chicken pieces (or a chicken carcass)
1 large onion, quartered
2 carrots, peeled and quartered
1 leek, sliced
4 celery stalks, sliced
1 bay leaf
½ tsp black peppercorns
½ tsp allspice berries
salt
3 quarts (3.5 liters) cold water
chopped fresh parsley
NOODLES
1 cup (125g) all-purpose flour, plus extra for
kneading
½ tsp salt
1 egg

ILLUSTRATED ON PAGE 166
THIS RICH, MEATY SOUP IS OFTEN SERVED ON CHRISTMAS DAY IN GERMANY, FOLLOWED BY ROAST GOOSE, HARE, OR VENISON.

SERVES 6

1 Heat the oil in a large pan. Add the bones, beef, and chicken and brown evenly. Alternatively, bake in a preheated oven at 400°F/200°C for 20 minutes, or until evenly browned, then transfer to a pan.

2 Add the vegetables, bay leaf, peppercorns, allspice, salt, and water to the pan. Bring to a boil, cover, and simmer for 3 hours.

3 Meanwhile, make the noodles. Sift the flour and salt into a bowl. Add the egg and mix together, adding enough water to make a firm dough.

4 Knead the dough on a lightly floured surface until smooth, then wrap in plastic wrap until required.

5 Strain the stock into a bowl and allow to cool. Skim off the fat, return the stock to the pan, and bring to a boil.

6 Roll the dough out until thin on a lightly floured surface. Cut the dough into shapes using a small star cutter. Drop the shapes directly into the soup and return to a boil. The noodles are cooked when they rise to the surface. Divide the noodles equally among individual plates and serve the soup hot, sprinkled with chopped parsley.

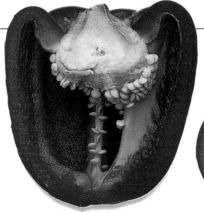

⊷ TOMATO & RED PEPPER SOUP ⊷

INGREDIENTS

3 red peppers, halved, cored, and seeded
2lb (1kg) ripe tomatoes, halved and seeded
2 red onions, quartered
2 garlic cloves, peeled
2 tbsp tomato paste
1 quart (1.25 liters) vegetable stock
salt and black pepper
3 tbsp light cream
croutons, cut from a slice of bread with a holly leaf cutter and fried in butter, to garnish

ILLUSTRATED ON PAGE 147
ROASTED SWEET RED PEPPERS GIVE THIS SOUP ITS INTENSE FLAVOR AND FESTIVE COLOR.

SERVES 6

1 Preheat the oven to 400°F/200°C. Place the peppers, tomatoes, onions, and garlic in a roasting pan and bake in the oven for 15–20 minutes, until the pepper skins have blistered.

2 Allow to cool slightly, then remove the skins from the peppers, tomatoes, and onions and place in a food processor with the garlic, tomato paste, and ⅔ cup (150ml) of the vegetable stock.

3 Blend the vegetable mixture until smooth, then pour into a large pan and add the remaining stock, salt, and pepper. Bring to a boil and simmer for 15 minutes.

4 Taste the soup and season if necessary. Serve in individual soup bowls with a swirl of cream and garnish with a few holly leaf croutons.

⊷ CHRISTMAS EVE SOUP ⊷

INGREDIENTS

MUSHROOM STOCK
3oz (90g) dried mushrooms, or
½lb (250g) fresh mushrooms, chopped
1 bay leaf
3½ cups (900ml) boiling water
BEET STOCK
2lb (1kg) small beets, peeled and chopped or grated
4 cups (1 liter) cold water
⅔ cup (150ml) red wine
½ tsp salt
black pepper
fresh rosemary sprigs, to garnish
DUMPLINGS
4 tbsp (60g) butter
1 onion, finely chopped
1 tsp chopped fresh marjoram
1 tbsp fresh white bread crumbs
salt and black pepper
1 cup (125g) all-purpose flour
1 tsp salt
1 egg
2–3 tsp cold water

ILLUSTRATED ON PAGE 147
CHRISTMAS EVE IN POLAND IS A FAST DAY, WHEN NO MEAT IS SERVED, BUT THERE IS PLENTY TO EAT, INCLUDING SOUP, NOODLES, FISH, AND PASTRIES. THIS BEET SOUP IS SERVED WITH STUFFED NOODLES KNOWN AS "LITTLE EARS."

SERVES 6

1 Place the mushrooms and bay leaf in a pan with the water. Soak for 2 hours if the mushrooms are dried.

2 Bring to a boil and simmer uncovered for 45–50 minutes, until the liquid has reduced to ⅔ cup (150ml). Strain the stock through a sieve into a bowl, pressing through all the liquid, and reserve the mushrooms.

3 Meanwhile, place the beets and water in a stainless steel pan and bring to a boil. Cover and simmer for 30 minutes, or until the beets are tender. Add the wine, salt, and pepper and cook for 10 minutes longer. Strain the beet stock through a fine sieve into a bowl, pressing through all the juices. Discard the beets.

4 To make the dumplings, melt the butter and sauté the onion until tender. Stir in the marjoram and the reserved mushrooms and cook until all the liquid has evaporated.

Remove from the heat and stir in the bread crumbs. Taste, season, and allow to cool.

5 Sift the flour into a bowl, add the salt, egg, and enough water to bind the mixture together, then knead into a soft dough.

6 Roll out the dough on a lightly floured surface to a paper-thin square and cut into about 60 x 1½ in (3.5cm) squares. Cover with a damp dish towel to prevent the dough from drying out. Knead the trimmings together, roll out, and again cut into squares.

7 Place a teaspoon of the mushroom filling in the center of each square and keep covered with a damp dish towel. Taking one square at a time, fold in half diagonally and seal the edges. Take the two points at the base of the triangle and pinch together. Place on a floured plate. Repeat with the remaining squares to make about 70 dumplings.

8 Cook a few dumplings at a time in a large pan of boiling salted water for 5 minutes. Remove with a slotted spoon and drain on paper towels. Place on a warm plate, cover with foil, and keep warm.

9 Pour the beet and mushroom stocks into a pan and bring to a boil. Taste for seasoning. Arrange a few dumplings in each warm bowl and ladle the soup over them. Garnish with rosemary sprigs.

CHRISTMAS EVE IN PROVENCE

THIS IS THE *GROS SOUPER* OF PROVENCE, served on Christmas Eve. It actually forms part of a fast, so fish is served, not meat, but it is still a sumptuous feast. The meal ends with the "thirteen desserts," symbolizing Christ and the twelve apostles. The centerpiece is a rich olive bread, surrounded by an assortment of fruit and nuts.

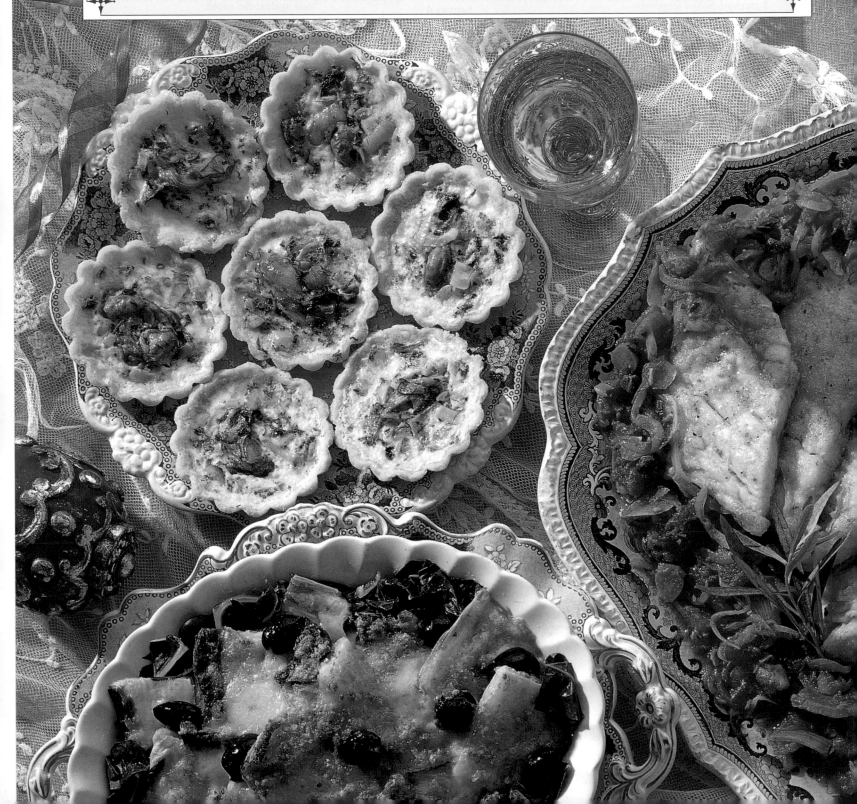

Salt Cod Provençal

INGREDIENTS

1½ lb (750g) salt cod
2 tbsp (15g) flour
black pepper
2 tbsp olive oil
2 tbsp (30g) butter
fresh herb sprig, to garnish
PROVENÇAL SAUCE
1 large onion, sliced
2 garlic cloves, crushed
1½ lb (750g) tomatoes, peeled and chopped
1 tbsp tomato paste
1 tbsp capers
1 tbsp gherkins
1 tbsp each chopped fresh tarragon,
thyme, and parsley

ILLUSTRATED ON PAGES 152–53
SALT COD MUST BE CAREFULLY PREPARED
TO BRING OUT ITS DELICATE FLAVOR. AT
CHRISTMAS, PROVENÇAL MARKETS
HAVE SPECIAL STALLS SELLING READY-
PREPARED SALT COD.

SERVES 6

1 Soak the cod in plenty of cold water, in a cool place, for 24 hours, changing the water three to four times.

2 Drain the fish and pat dry with paper towels. Cut into 6 even-sized pieces, discarding the fins and bones. Season the flour with black pepper. Dip the fish pieces in the flour until evenly coated on both sides.

3 Heat the oil and butter in a large skillet. Add half the pieces of fish and cook until golden brown on both sides. Remove the fish with a slotted spoon and drain on paper towels. Keep warm while the remaining pieces of fish are cooked.

4 To make the Provençal sauce, add the onion and garlic to the skillet and cook for 2–3 minutes, until tender but not browned. Stir in the tomatoes and tomato paste and bring to a boil. Cook gently for 2–3 minutes, then stir in the capers, gherkins, and herbs and season with black pepper.

5 Pour the sauce onto a large warm serving dish and carefully arrange the fish on top. Garnish with a sprig of fresh herbs.

Poached Salmon with Hollandaise Sauce

INGREDIENTS

6 lb (2.75kg) whole salmon, cleaned
2–3 sprigs of fresh dill
2 bay leaves
4 shallots, quartered
1 tbsp black peppercorns
1 tbsp salt
¼ cucumber, thinly sliced
1 lemon, thinly sliced
fresh dill sprigs, to garnish
HOLLANDAISE SAUCE
8 egg yolks
⅓ cup (90ml) lemon juice
salt and black pepper
¾ lb (375g) unsalted butter
1 bunch watercress (optional)
1 bunch fresh basil (optional)

A WONDERFUL CENTERPIECE FOR A
CHRISTMAS BUFFET, THIS POPULAR SALMON
DISH IS EASY TO PREPARE. FOR EXTRA
COLOR, SERVE WITH A GREEN
HOLLANDAISE SAUCE.

SERVES 10–12

1 Wash the salmon, dry with paper towels, and place the dill sprigs in the cavity. Arrange the salmon in a fish poacher or large roasting pan. Add the bay leaves, shallots, peppercorns, and salt, and pour in enough water to cover the salmon. Cover with nonstick baking parchment, and then with the fish poacher lid or foil.

2 Bring slowly to a boil on top of the stove, then turn off the heat and let stand for 30 minutes. If the salmon is to be served cold, allow to stand until the water is completely cold.

3 Meanwhile, make the hollandaise sauce. Place the egg yolks, lemon juice, salt, and pepper in a blender or food processor and blend until smooth.

4 Heat the butter over low heat until it is bubbling, but do not allow it to brown. With the machine running, slowly add half the melted butter to the egg yolk mixture in

a steady stream. Blend for about 10 seconds, until it is well incorporated.

5 Add the remaining butter in a steady stream and continue to blend until the mixture is pale and has thickened. Taste for seasoning, then pour the sauce into a warm sauceboat or bowl. Keep warm in a bain marie or over a pan of warm water.

6 To make green hollandaise, strip the leaves from the watercress. Add the watercress leaves and basil to the sauce in the blender when all the butter has been added. Process until smooth.

7 Drain off the liquid from the fish poacher. Carefully lift out the salmon, place on a large serving dish, and keep warm. Cut the skin neatly around the head and tail and carefully peel off the skin, including the fins, leaving the head and tail intact.

8 Arrange overlapping cucumber slices along the backbone of the salmon and alternate lemon and cucumber slices around the head. Garnish with sprigs of dill and serve with the hollandaise sauce.

CARP WITH SWEET & SOUR SAUCE

INGREDIENTS

4lb (2kg) carp, cleaned and scaled
2 tbsp (30g) unsalted butter
2 carrots, chopped
1 leek, sliced
4 celery stalks, sliced
2 onions, quartered
2 bay leaves
2 sprigs of fresh thyme
1 tsp allspice berries
2 strips of lemon zest
salt and black pepper
4 cups (1 liter) water
2½ cups (600ml) dark ale
⅓ cup (60g) raisins
2oz (60g) ginger spiced cake or cookies
chopped fresh parsley, lemon wedges, and
toasted sliced almonds, to garnish

THIS GERMAN RECIPE DATES FROM THE MIDDLE AGES, WHEN MONASTERIES HAD SPECIAL PONDS FOR BREEDING CARP. THEY WOULD START TO FATTEN THE FISH FOR CHRISTMAS ON ST. BARTHOLOMEW'S DAY (AUGUST 24).

SERVES 6

1 Wash the carp and dry on paper towels. Melt the butter in a large ovenproof dish or casserole, add the carrots, leek, celery, and onion, and cook for 4–5 minutes, until the vegetables have softened, stirring occasionally. Add the bay leaves, thyme, allspice berries, lemon zest, salt, and pepper.

2 Arrange the fish on top of the bed of vegetables and pour over the water and dark ale. Bring to a boil on top of the stove, then cover and cook very gently over a low heat for 15–20 minutes, or until the fin pulls out easily.

3 Remove the fish carefully, using two spatulas, and place on a warm serving dish. Keep warm while you make the sauce.

4 Strain the stock from the vegetables into a pan. Add the raisins. Crumble the cake or cookies and stir the crumbs into the pan. Bring to a boil and simmer for 1 minute, until slightly thickened. Spoon the sauce over the fish and garnish with chopped parsley, lemon wedges, and toasted sliced almonds.

TROUT WITH DARK FRUIT SAUCE

INGREDIENTS

2 tbsp (30g) unsalted butter
6 trout, cleaned and trimmed
salt and black pepper
finely grated zest of 1 lemon
2 tbsp chopped fresh parsley
SAUCE
¼ cup (60g) sugar
2½ cups (600ml) water
4 tbsp red wine vinegar
2 bay leaves
2 tbsp blueberry jelly
¼ cup (60g) pitted prunes, chopped
¼ cup (60g) dried apricots, chopped
grated zest and juice of 1 lemon
lemon wedges and fresh parsley sprigs, to garnish

THIS FISH RECIPE WITH ITS UNUSUAL SAUCE COMES FROM THE CZECH REPUBLIC. THE CONTRAST OF THE BRIGHT PINK TROUT AGAINST THE DARK FRUIT SAUCE MAKES A VERY APPEALING DISH.

SERVES 6

1 Melt the butter in a shallow flameproof dish. Sprinkle the trout with salt, pepper, lemon zest, and parsley, then add to the dish and cook for a few minutes on each side to brown evenly.

2 To make the sauce, place the sugar and 1 tablespoon of the water in a pan. Heat gently until the sugar dissolves, then boil rapidly until the syrup turns a rich brown.

3 Add the vinegar to the syrup and stir to dissolve the caramel. Stir in the remaining water, bay leaves, blueberry jelly, prunes, apricots, lemon zest, and juice. Bring the sauce to a boil and pour over the trout in the flameproof dish. Cover and cook gently for 5 minutes, until the fish is tender.

4 Lift out the trout onto a board and carefully remove the skin, leaving the head and tail intact. Arrange the trout on a serving dish and keep warm.

5 Bring the sauce to a boil and cook until it has reduced and thickened. Serve the trout on individual plates and spoon the sauce around. Garnish with lemon wedges and parsley sprigs.

DIP-IN-THE-POT CRUSTED HAM

INGREDIENTS
6–8lb (3–4kg) shank end salt-cured ham
2 large onions, sliced
2 carrots, sliced
1 leek, sliced
4 celery stalks, sliced
2 bay leaves
½ tsp peppercorns
4 cloves
2½ cups (600ml) beer
1lb (500g) smoked pork sausages
rye bread, to serve
CRUST
2 cups (250g) rye or whole wheat flour
4½ cups (500g) fresh white bread crumbs
½ cup (125g) light brown sugar
2 tbsp (30g) each chopped fresh parsley and dill
2 tbsp dry mustard
2 eggs, beaten
6 tbsp (90ml) clear honey
2 tbsp finely chopped fresh parsley

THE SWEDISH RITUAL KNOWN AS "DIPPING IN THE POT" DATES BACK TO THE TIME WHEN NOTHING COULD BE WASTED, AND BROTH LEFT OVER FROM COOKING THE CHRISTMAS HAM WAS NO EXCEPTION. EVERYONE DIPS A PIECE OF RYE BREAD INTO THE BROTH.

SERVES 6–8

1 Soak the ham in cold water for 12 hours, changing the water 2–3 times. Drain well.

2 Place the ham in a large saucepan, cover with water, and bring to a boil. Remove the ham and pour off the water.

3 Place the onions, carrots, leek, celery, bay leaves, peppercorns, and cloves in the pan. Add the ham, beer, and sausages and enough water to cover. Bring to a boil, cover, and cook very gently for 2 hours. Let the ham and sausages cool overnight in the broth.

4 To make the crust, mix the flour, bread crumbs, sugar, parsley, dill, and mustard in a bowl until evenly blended. Mix in just enough of the beaten egg to bind the mixture together.

5 Preheat the oven to 400°F/200°C. Remove the ham from the broth and drain well. Peel off the skin and score the fat with a sharp knife. Warm the honey and brush evenly over the ham.

6 Press the crumb mixture over the ham until evenly covered. Place the ham in a roasting pan and bake for 40–50 minutes, or until the crust is golden brown. Allow to cool.

7 Remove the sausages from the broth. Strain the broth through a sieve, pushing through the vegetables with a wooden spoon. Return the broth to the pan and bring to a boil. Adjust the seasoning and sprinkle with chopped parsley.

8 Arrange the ham on a serving dish with the sausages. Serve with the broth and a plate of rye bread cubes for dipping.

ROAST VENISON WITH APPLES & PEARS

INGREDIENTS
4–6 lb (2–3kg) saddle of venison
2 tbsp olive oil
4 tbsp (60g) butter
2 onions, sliced
1 leek, sliced
4 celery stalks, sliced
½ cup (60g) flour
¼ lb (125g) fatback, cut into strips
4 pears, halved and cored
4 red apples, halved and cored
juice of 2 lemons
2 tsp clear honey
4 tbsp brandy
⅔ cup (150ml) sour cream
sprigs of fresh rosemary, to garnish
MARINADE
2½ cups (600ml) dry red wine
2½ cups (600ml) cold water
1 tsp each whole cloves, peppercorns, and juniper berries
1 bay leaf
2 tsp salt

DEER ARE STILL HUNTED IN THE FORESTS OF GERMANY DURING THE SEASON. AFTERWARD, THE SPOILS ARE HONORED WITH A TORCHLIT CEREMONY AND A SPECIAL SALUTE FROM THE HUNTING HORNS.

SERVES 6–8

1 To make the marinade, place the wine, water, cloves, peppercorns, juniper berries, bay leaf, and salt in a stainless steel pan. Bring the marinade to a boil, then let cool to room temperature.

2 Place the venison in a large dish or stainless steel roasting pan. Pour over the marinade, cover, and leave at room temperature for 6 hours, turning frequently, or in the refrigerator for 2 days.

3 Preheat the oven to 350°F/180°C. Pour the oil into a roasting pan and heat in the oven until very hot.

4 Remove the venison, reserving the marinade, and pat the meat dry with paper towels. Add to the roasting pan and brown on all sides, turning frequently.

5 Meanwhile, melt the butter in a large saucepan and add the onion, leek, and celery. Cook quickly, stirring occasionally, until the vegetables are lightly browned.

6 Add the flour and cook over low heat, stirring until golden brown, taking care not to burn the flour. Stir in the marinade, bring to a boil, and remove from the heat.

7 Remove the venison from the roasting pan, pour in the vegetable mixture, and place the venison on top. Cover with the strips of fatback. Roast in the oven for 1½ hours, basting with the marinade, until the meat is tender and slightly pink.

8 Meanwhile, cut the pear and apple halves into thin slices, but not all the way through, keeping the fruit intact. Place each piece of fruit on a square of foil, pour over the lemon juice, and drizzle with honey. Seal the parcels, place on a baking sheet, and bake in the oven for 5–10 minutes, until tender.

9 Place the venison on a warm serving dish and remove the strips of fatback. Strain the marinade and vegetables through a fine sieve, pressing out all the juices. Bring to a boil, add the brandy and cream, taste, and season. Pour some of the sauce around the venison and serve the remainder in a warm sauceboat. Garnish the venison with the pear and apple halves, and sprigs of rosemary.

Standing Ribs of Beef with a Mustard Crust

INGREDIENTS
*6lb (3kg) rib roast of beef, chine bone removed
(6-bone)*
MUSTARD CRUST
*2 tbsp oil
2 cups (175g) fresh bread crumbs
1 onion, finely chopped
2 tbsp chopped fresh oregano
1 tbsp mixed peppercorns, crushed
½ tsp salt
4 tbsp coarse-grain mustard*

THE ROAST BEEF OF OLD ENGLAND REMAINS A CHERISHED NATIONAL DISH. ORIGINALLY, LARGE CUTS OF BEEF WERE SPIT-ROASTED OVER AN OPEN FIRE, AND YORKSHIRE PUDDINGS WERE COOKED UNDERNEATH IN THE BEEF JUICES. IN THIS RECIPE THE BEEF IS GIVEN A CRISP COATING TO KEEP THE MEAT MOIST AND FULL OF FLAVOR.

SERVES 6

1 Preheat the oven to 425°F/220°C. To make the mustard crust, stir the oil, bread crumbs, onion, oregano, peppercorns, and salt in a bowl until evenly mixed. Add the mustard to the bowl and stir until the mixture begins to bind together.

2 Press the mixture evenly over the flesh side of the ribs, leaving the bones uncovered. Place the ribs of beef in a roasting pan with the mustard crust side up.

3 Roast the beef in the oven for 30 minutes, then reduce the heat to 375°F/190°C and cook for another hour, or until the meat is cooked to your taste, allowing 20 minutes per 1lb (500g) for rare beef, 25-30 minutes for medium, and 30-35 minutes for well-done. Cover the crust with foil if it becomes too brown.

4 Transfer the meat to a warm serving dish and leave to firm up for 15 minutes, making it easier to carve.

5 Cut into slices to serve – the crust will crumble as it is sliced. Serve a little crust with each portion and accompany the beef with Yorkshire puddings, roast potatoes, and vegetables such as Brussels sprouts.

Roast Lamb

INGREDIENTS
*6–7lb (3–3.5kg) leg of lamb
5 whole garlic bulbs
sprigs of fresh rosemary, thyme, and parsley
salt and black pepper
2 tbsp clear honey
1 tbsp lemon juice
lemon wedges and fresh parsley sprigs,
to garnish*

ILLUSTRATED ON PAGE 173
THIS CELEBRATION ROAST FROM NORWAY SHOWS A DEFINITE FRENCH INFLUENCE, WITH THE FLAVORS OF ROASTED GARLIC AND HERBS.

SERVES 6

1 Preheat the oven to 375°F/190°C. Place the leg of lamb in a roasting pan. Divide one garlic bulb into cloves and peel and slice the cloves.

2 Using a sharp knife, make small incisions all over the lamb. Insert alternate sprigs of herbs and slivers of garlic until the lamb is evenly covered.

3 Roast the lamb in the oven for 1¾ hours, then brush with the honey and lemon juice. Place the remaining garlic bulbs around the roast and cook for 30–40 minutes longer, until the lamb is tender and slightly pink inside.

4 Arrange on a serving dish and garnish with lemon wedges, parsley sprigs, and the bulbs of garlic, divided into cloves.

STUFFED QUAIL WITH GRAPES

INGREDIENTS
8 oven-ready quail
4 tbsp olive oil
salt and black pepper
1lb (500g) red or white seedless grapes
1 cup (250ml) chicken stock
grape leaves, to garnish (optional)
STUFFING
2 tbsp (30g) butter
2 shallots, chopped
1 garlic clove, crushed
4 chicken livers, chopped
1 cup (60g) sun-dried tomatoes, chopped
2 tbsp chopped fennel
salt and black pepper
3 tbsp Marsala
1 cup (60g) fresh white bread crumbs

AN ELEGANT RECIPE FROM TUSCANY, SUITABLE FOR PIGEONS AS WELL AS QUAIL.

SERVES 4–6

1 To make the stuffing, melt the butter in a skillet, add the shallots and garlic, and cook for 1–2 minutes, until tender. Add the livers and sauté for a few minutes.

2 Add the sun-dried tomatoes, fennel, salt, pepper, and Marsala. Bring to a boil and remove from the heat. Stir in the fresh bread crumbs and let cool.

3 Place a quail on a board, breast side down, and remove the backbone by cutting down each side with kitchen scissors. Turn the bird over and flatten by pressing down on the breastbone with the heel of your hand. Repeat with the remaining quail.

4 Preheat the oven to 375°F/190°C. Loosen the skin of the quail from the flesh with your fingers and spoon the stuffing beneath the skin. Spread the stuffing evenly over the flesh of the quail and pull the skin tight to flatten it. Hold the legs and wings in place with toothpicks and arrange the quail in a large roasting pan. Brush the skins with olive oil and season.

5 Place two thirds of the grapes in a food processor and blend until smooth. Strain the grape mixture through a sieve and pour over the quail with the stock.

6 Roast the quail in the preheated oven for 30–40 minutes, until tender, covering with foil if they brown too quickly.

7 To serve, arrange the quail on a warmed serving dish, strain the sauce, and pour over. Garnish with small bunches of the remaining grapes and a few grape leaves, if available. Serve with Glazed Florentine Fennel (see page 163).

ROAST GOOSE WITH APPLE & NUT STUFFING

INGREDIENTS
8–10lb (4–5kg) oven-ready goose with giblets
salt and black pepper
6 slices goose fat or fatback
3 red apples, halved and cored
3 green apples, halved and cored
juice of 1 lemon
2 tbsp clear honey
1 cup (125g) toasted almonds, to garnish
fresh rosemary sprigs, to garnish
STUFFING
4 tbsp (60g) butter
1 cup (175g) raisins
4 onions, chopped
3 cooking apples, peeled, cored, and coarsely chopped
1 cup (125g) blanched almonds, chopped
2¼ cups (250g) fresh white bread crumbs
1 tbsp each chopped fresh parsley, sage, and thyme
1 tsp ground cloves

ILLUSTRATED ON PAGES 166–67
GOOSE STUFFED WITH APPLES AND NUTS IS THE TRADITIONAL CHRISTMAS DAY BIRD IN GERMANY. THE USUAL ACCOMPANIMENTS ARE RED CABBAGE AND POTATO DUMPLINGS.

SERVES 6–8

1 Preheat the oven to 400°F/200°C. Wipe the goose and remove any excess fat from inside. Place the giblets in a pan with water to cover, and season. Bring to a boil, cover, and simmer for 45 minutes. Reserve the stock for gravy. Chop the liver for stuffing.

2 To make the stuffing, melt the butter and cook the raisins, onion, and apple for 2–3 minutes, stirring. Remove from the heat and add the almonds, bread crumbs, herbs, cloves, and chopped liver.

3 Stuff the neck end of the goose, securing the skin flap underneath the wing tips, and place the remainder in the body cavity of the goose or make stuffing balls. Secure the tail end with skewers and truss the goose neatly with string to hold the wings and legs in position, close to the body.

4 Cover the breast with goose fat or fatback and tie on securely with string. Sprinkle with salt and pepper. Place a rack in a large roasting pan and lay the goose breast side down. Cook in the oven for 30 minutes, then reduce the heat to 350°F/180°C.

5 Remove the goose from the oven and prick the skin around the neck, wings, thighs, back, and lower breast. Return to the oven for 3–3½ hours longer, removing excess fat and basting regularly. Add stuffing balls 30 minutes from the end of the cooking time.

6 Test the goose by piercing the thigh with a sharp knife – the juices should run pale yellow, not pink. Let the goose rest for 15 minutes before carving.

7 Meanwhile, thinly slice the apple halves, but not all the way through. Place each half on a square of foil, drizzle with lemon juice and honey, and add a sprig of rosemary. Seal the parcels and bake in the oven for 10–15 minutes, then unwrap carefully.

8 Serve the goose garnished with the apples, stuffing balls, if using, toasted almonds, and sprigs of rosemary.

Roast Turkey with Cornbread Stuffing

Ingredients

12lb (5.5kg) oven-ready turkey

1lb (500g) bacon

*5–6 clementine shells filled with cranberries
and blueberries, slices of spiced, buttered
pumpkin, roasted chestnuts, and sage sprigs,
to garnish*

Cornbread Stuffing

2 tbsp (30g) butter

3 onions, finely chopped

2 garlic cloves, chopped

6 celery stalks, chopped

½lb (250g) pork sausage meat

*2 x 8½oz (240g) cans whole peeled chestnuts,
finely chopped*

8oz (250g) cornbread, crumbled

*1 tbsp each chopped fresh parsley, sage,
and thyme*

salt and black pepper

1 tsp ground cinnamon

zest and juice of 1 orange

1 egg

ILLUSTRATED ON PAGES 160–61

ROAST TURKEY IS OFTEN SERVED IN NORTH
AMERICA AT CHRISTMAS. CORNBREAD IS A
FAVORITE STUFFING, AND QUITE DELICIOUS.

Serves 6–8

1 To make the stuffing, melt the butter in a
pan, add the onion, garlic, and celery, and
cook for 2 minutes, stirring occasionally. Add
the sausage meat and cook over high heat
until lightly brown. Remove from the heat.

2 In a bowl, mix together the chestnuts,
cornbread, parsley, sage, thyme, salt,
pepper, cinnamon, orange zest, and juice.
Add the sausage mixture. Stir until evenly
blended, then mix in the egg.

3 Place a quarter of the stuffing in the neck
end of the turkey, pull over the skin flap,
and secure under the turkey using a trussing
needle and string.

4 Fill the cavity of the turkey with the
remaining stuffing, pull the skin over the

tail, and secure with the needle and string.
Alternatively, make small stuffing balls.

5 Truss the turkey, using the needle and
string to secure the wings and legs close to
the body, and place in a roasting pan. Cover
with bacon slices to keep the meat moist
while cooking. Chill until ready to cook.

6 Preheat the oven to 375°F/190°C. Roast
the turkey for 2 hours, then remove the
bacon and cover with foil.

7 Return the turkey to the oven for 2 hours
longer. Add stuffing balls 30 minutes
before the end. To test for doneness, pierce
with a sharp knife between the legs and body
of the turkey – the juices should run clear.

8 Let the turkey stand for 20 minutes before
removing the trussing string. Place on a
warm serving dish and garnish with
clementine shells filled with cranberries
and blueberries, stuffing balls, if using, slices
of spiced, buttered pumpkin, roasted
chestnuts, and sage sprigs.

Plum, Lemon, & Herb Stuffing

Ingredients

2 tbsp (30g) butter

2 onions, finely chopped

*1lb (500g) plums, halved,
pitted, and sliced*

grated zest and juice of 1 large lemon

1 tbsp clear honey

*1 tbsp each chopped fresh thyme,
oregano, and parsley*

1 tsp salt

½ tsp freshly ground black pepper

2 cups (250g) medium oatmeal

3 cups (375g) fresh white bread crumbs

2 eggs, beaten

THIS LIGHT, TANGY STUFFING IS ENOUGH TO
STUFF A 12LB (5.5KG) TURKEY. IF FRESH PLUMS
ARE UNAVAILABLE, USE 1LB (500G) OF
CANNED PLUMS, WELL DRAINED.

1 Melt the butter in a medium-sized pan,
add the onion and plums, and cook over
low heat for 5 minutes, until almost tender.
Stir in the lemon zest and juice, the honey,
herbs, salt, and pepper.

2 Mix the oatmeal and bread crumbs in a
large bowl and add the onion mixture and
eggs. Stir until evenly blended, then cover and
chill until ready to use.

Chestnut & Cranberry Stuffing

Ingredients

2 tbsp (30g) butter

2 onions, finely chopped

2 cups (250g) cranberries

1 tsp ground cinnamon

grated zest and juice of 1 orange

*2 x 8½oz (240g) cans whole, peeled chestnuts,
finely chopped*

2¼ cups (250g) fresh white bread crumbs

salt and black pepper

1 egg

A STUFFING WITH A NUTTY FLAVOR AND
TEXTURE; MAKES ENOUGH TO STUFF A
12LB (5.5KG) TURKEY.

1 Melt the butter in a medium-sized pan,
add the onion, and cook over low heat for
2 minutes. Add the cranberries, cinnamon,
orange zest, and juice and cook for 2 minutes.
Remove from the heat.

2 Place the chopped chestnuts, bread
crumbs, salt, and pepper in a large bowl

and mix well. Stir in the cranberry and
orange mixture and the egg, mixing until
well blended. Cover the stuffing with plastic
wrap and chill until ready to use.

NORTH AMERICAN CHRISTMAS LUNCH

SINCE THE DAYS OF THE EARLY AMERICAN SETTLERS, roast turkey has been served as a celebration dish. Cornbread stuffing and a sweet-sour cranberry sauce are the usual accompaniments, other favorites being mashed potatoes flavored with garlic and herbs, stuffed onions, and creamed spinach. Special desserts include crunchy pecan pie, rich, sweet, and dark, and a creamy, tangy cheesecake topped with fresh blueberries.

Roast Turkey p.159 & center
Cranberry Sauce p.165 & top
Stuffed Onions p.164 & top left
Garlic & Herb Potatoes p.162 & left
Creamed Spinach p.164 & right

Pecan Pie p.171 & right
Blueberry Cheesecake
p.171 & right

ACCOMPANIMENTS

ROAST POTATOES AND BRUSSELS SPROUTS are often served with the Christmas meal, but there are plenty of alternatives to excite a jaded palate. Try the garlicky mashed potatoes served with the American turkey, or wickedly rich gratin potatoes, cooked with cream, Gruyère cheese, and egg.

Chard, the spinachlike vegetable beloved by the French, would make a tasty change, cooked au gratin, as would glazed Florentine fennel, flavored with pine nuts, garlic, and ginger. Even humble Brussels sprouts take on a new lease on life when tossed with toasted almonds, thyme, and lemon.

POTATO DUMPLINGS

INGREDIENTS
2lb (1kg) medium-sized potatoes, scrubbed
salt and black pepper
¼ cup (30g) flour
2 tbsp (30g) semolina
1½ tsp freshly ground nutmeg
2 eggs, beaten
2 tbsp toasted bread crumbs

THESE LIGHT, FLUFFY DUMPLINGS ARE ONE OF THE TRADITIONAL ACCOMPANIMENTS FOR ROAST GOOSE.

MAKES 12

1 Boil the potatoes in salted water for about 10 minutes, until almost tender. Drain, leave until cool enough to handle, then peel.

2 Mix together in a bowl the flour, semolina, salt, pepper, and nutmeg.

3 Grate the potatoes coarsely and add to the bowl. Mix in lightly.

4 Add the eggs and mix together to form a soft dough, adding more flour if necessary. Using floured hands, shape the mixture into 20 round balls.

5 Cook the dumplings in boiling salted water for 8-10 minutes, or until they rise to the surface. Remove with a slotted spoon and drain on paper towels.

6 Arrange the dumplings on a warm serving plate and sprinkle with toasted bread crumbs, or roll them individually in the bread crumbs to coat evenly.

SWISS FRIED POTATOES

INGREDIENTS
8 medium-sized baking potatoes
salt and black pepper
1 tbsp chopped fresh parsley
3 tbsp olive oil
2 tbsp (30g) butter
sprigs of fresh parsley, to garnish

OTHERWISE KNOWN AS RÖSTI, THESE GOLDEN BROWN POTATO CAKES ARE A SWISS SPECIALTY.

SERVES 6

1 Boil the potatoes in salted water for about 10 minutes, until almost tender, then drain. When cool enough to handle, peel, and place the cooked potatoes in a bowl. Cover and chill for 1 hour.

2 Grate the potatoes on a coarse grater into a bowl. Add pepper and the chopped parsley and mix together.

3 Heat the oil and butter in a nonstick skillet. Place heaping tablespoonfuls of the potato mixture in the pan, evenly spaced apart. Press the potatoes into flat shapes using a spatula, and cook for 2–3 minutes, until golden brown underneath.

4 Turn each potato cake once and cook for another 2–3 minutes to brown the other side. Remove with a spatula and keep warm while cooking the remaining mixture. Arrange on a warm serving plate and garnish with sprigs of parsley.

GARLIC & HERB POTATOES

INGREDIENTS
3lb (1.5kg) potatoes, peeled and cut into chunks
6 garlic cloves, peeled
salt and black pepper
4 tbsp (60g) butter
¼ cup (60ml) milk
2 tbsp chopped fresh parsley

ILLUSTRATED ON PAGE 160
IN NORTH AMERICA, SMOOTH, CREAMY, GARLIC-FLAVORED POTATOES ARE SERVED WITH THE CHRISTMAS TURKEY.

SERVES 6

1 Bring the potatoes and garlic to a boil in salted water. Cover and simmer gently for 10 minutes, or until the potatoes are tender.

2 Drain the potatoes and garlic, add pepper, butter, and milk, and mash until smooth and creamy. Stir in the parsley and pile onto a warm serving dish. Serve with roast turkey.

GRATIN POTATOES

INGREDIENTS

4 tbsp (60g) butter
2lb (1kg) potatoes, peeled
salt and black pepper
grated nutmeg
6oz (175g) Gruyère, grated
⅔ cup (150ml) light cream or milk
1 egg

ILLUSTRATED ON PAGE 172
THIS CREAMY POTATO DISH MAKES THE
PERFECT ACCOMPANIMENT TO A LARGE ROAST,
SUCH AS BEEF OR LEG OF LAMB.

SERVES 6

1 Preheat the oven to 375°F/190°C. Lightly butter a shallow, ovenproof dish.

2 Using a large grater or the slicer on a food processor, thinly slice the potatoes.

3 Arrange a layer of potato slices in the dish and sprinkle with salt, pepper, nutmeg, and a little grated cheese. Continue to layer the potatoes and cheese, reserving a little cheese for the top, until the dish is filled. Beat together the cream and egg and pour over the top of the dish.

4 Sprinkle the top with the reserved cheese. Bake for 40–50 minutes, or until the top is golden brown and the potatoes are tender.

CARAMELIZED CARROTS & ONIONS

INGREDIENTS

24 baby carrots, peeled
24 small onions
½ cup (125g) superfine sugar
¼ cup water
¼ lb (125g) unsalted butter
1 tbsp lemon juice
1 tbsp chopped fresh parsley

ILLUSTRATED ON PAGE 173
CARAMELIZED VEGETABLES ACCOMPANY THE
CHRISTMAS ROAST IN NORWAY.

SERVES 6

1 Place the carrots and onions in separate pans of boiling salted water. Cover and simmer for 5–10 minutes, until tender. Drain and cool slightly, then peel the onions.

2 Gently heat the sugar and water, stirring occasionally, until the sugar has dissolved.

3 Boil rapidly until the bubbles subside and a golden brown syrup forms. Add the butter and stir to blend evenly, then stir in the lemon juice until smooth.

4 Place the carrots and onions in the caramel and toss to coat evenly. Place on a warm serving plate and sprinkle with chopped parsley. Serve hot.

GLAZED FLORENTINE FENNEL

INGREDIENTS

⅔ cup (150ml) vegetable stock
3 fennel bulbs, quartered
1 tbsp olive oil
2 tbsp (30g) unsalted butter
2 tbsp pine nuts
2 red onions, cut into wedges
2 garlic cloves, sliced
½ in (1cm) fresh ginger, peeled and cut into strips

A WONDERFUL MIXTURE OF COLORS
AND FLAVORS IS REFLECTED IN
THIS ITALIAN RECIPE.

SERVES 6

1 Place the stock in a saucepan and bring to a boil. Add the fennel quarters and cook for 2 minutes. Remove with a slotted spoon and keep warm. Reserve the stock.

2 Heat the oil and butter in a skillet, add the pine nuts and brown lightly. Remove with a slotted spoon.

3 Add the onion, garlic, ginger, and fennel quarters to the pan. Cook for 1–2 minutes, turning the vegetables gently. Pour in the stock and cook quickly for 1 minute. Arrange the fennel and onions in a serving dish and sprinkle with the pine nuts.

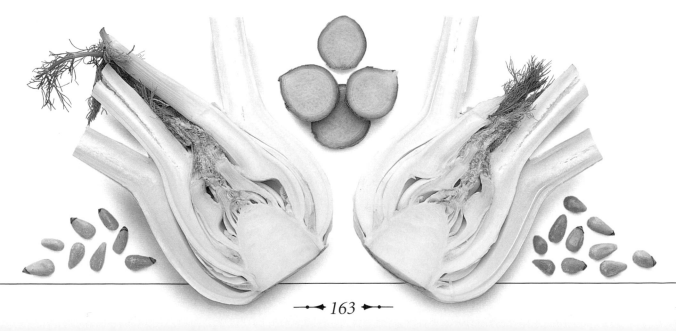

STUFFED ONIONS

INGREDIENTS
6 medium-sized white onions, peeled
2 tbsp olive oil
1 garlic clove, crushed
8 oz (250g) wild mushrooms, chopped
2 tbsp chopped fresh oregano
salt and black pepper
2 tbsp fresh white bread crumbs
⅔ cup (150ml) vegetable stock
2 tbsp dry sherry
fresh parsley sprigs, to garnish

ILLUSTRATED ON PAGE 160
TRY THE MILD, SWEET FLAVOR OF WHITE ONIONS, FILLED WITH A MIXTURE OF WILD MUSHROOMS AND HERBS.

SERVES 6

1 Preheat the oven to 400°F/200°C. Place the onions in a pan of boiling water for 5 minutes, then drain well and cool.

2 Scoop out the center of each onion, leaving the base and shell intact. Finely chop the centers.

3 Heat the oil in a skillet and quickly cook the chopped onion, garlic, and mushrooms for 1–2 minutes, until tender. Stir in the oregano, salt, pepper, and bread crumbs.

4 Fill the cavity of each onion with the mushroom mixture. Place the remaining stuffing in an ovenproof dish and arrange the onions on top.

5 Pour the stock and sherry into the dish and bake for 30 minutes, or until the onions are tender. Arrange on a warm serving dish and garnish with parsley sprigs.

CREAMED SPINACH

INGREDIENTS
3lb (1.5kg) spinach
SAUCE
2 tbsp (30g) butter
¼ cup (30g) flour
salt and black pepper
⅔ cup (150ml) milk
½ tsp freshly grated nutmeg
2 tbsp heavy cream

ILLUSTRATED ON PAGE 161
FRESHLY COOKED SPINACH IS SERVED WITH A CREAMY SAUCE FLAVORED WITH NUTMEG.

SERVES 6

1 Cook the spinach in ⅔ cup (150ml) boiling water for 1 minute, then drain well and chop fine.

2 To make the sauce, place the butter, flour, salt, pepper, and milk in a small pan.

Whisk continuously over moderate heat until the sauce thickens.

3 Simmer the sauce over low heat for 2 minutes, stirring occasionally. Add the nutmeg and spinach and stir until well blended and heated through.

4 Add the cream, stir well, and spoon into a warm serving dish.

CHARD AU GRATIN

INGREDIENTS
2lb (1kg) chard, trimmed
2 tbsp olive oil
1 garlic clove, crushed
¼ cup (30g) flour
⅔ cup (150ml) vegetable stock
⅔ cup (150ml) white wine
salt and black pepper
½ tsp freshly grated nutmeg
1 tbsp black pitted olives, halved
2oz (60g) Gruyère cheese, grated
2 tbsp fresh white bread crumbs

ILLUSTRATED ON PAGE 152
THIS WONDERFUL LEAFY GREEN VEGETABLE IS A FAVORITE WITH THE FRENCH.

SERVES 6

1 Slice the chard into bite-sized lengths. Heat the oil in a large skillet.

2 Add the garlic and chard and sauté quickly for 1 minute, stirring all the time. Remove the chard with a slotted spoon and set aside.

3 Stir in the flour, stock, wine, salt, pepper, and nutmeg. Bring to a boil and cook for

2 minutes. Add the chard and olives and stir to mix well.

4 Put the chard mixture into a flameproof dish and sprinkle with the cheese and bread crumbs. Place under a hot broiler until lightly browned and bubbling.

BRUSSELS SPROUTS WITH ALMONDS

INGREDIENTS
1½lb (750g) Brussels sprouts
salt and black pepper
2 tbsp (30g) butter
½ cup (60g) sliced almonds
1 tbsp chopped fresh thyme
2 tsp lemon zest

IF IMAGINATIVELY COOKED, THIS POPULAR VEGETABLE CAN BE SERVED IN STYLE AT A CHRISTMAS MEAL. TRY TOSSING THEM WITH ALMONDS, THYME, AND LEMON.

SERVES 6

1 Quarter the Brussels sprouts if large, otherwise cut them in half. Bring a large pan of salted water to a boil. Add the sprouts,

cover, and simmer for 5 minutes, until they are just tender and bright green. Drain well.

2 Meanwhile, melt the butter in a skillet, add the almonds, and stir-fry until they are golden brown.

3 Stir in the thyme, lemon zest, and pepper, add the sprouts, and toss well to coat evenly. Place in a warm serving dish.

❧ RED CABBAGE ❧

INGREDIENTS

1 red cabbage, finely shredded
⅔ cup (150ml) red wine vinegar
2 tbsp (30g) sugar
1 tsp salt
4 whole cloves
1 bay leaf
2 tbsp (30g) goose fat or 2 tbsp vegetable oil
2 red onions, sliced
1 cooking apple, peeled, cored, and sliced
⅔ cup (150ml) giblet stock
4 tbsp red currant jelly
⅔ cup (150ml) red wine

ILLUSTRATED ON PAGE 166
SPICY SWEET AND SOUR RED CABBAGE IS A
FAVORITE WINTER DISH ALL OVER EUROPE. IT
IS A TRADITIONAL ACCOMPANIMENT TO ROAST
GOOSE, AND IS OFTEN COOKED IN GOOSE FAT.

SERVES 6

1 Place the cabbage, vinegar, sugar, salt, cloves, and bay leaf in a bowl and mix to blend evenly.

2 Heat the goose fat or oil in a flameproof casserole, add the onions and apple, and cook until lightly browned, stirring.

3 Stir in the cabbage and stock and bring to a boil. Cover and cook gently for about 30 minutes, until the cabbage is tender and most of the stock has evaporated. Add more stock or water if necessary.

4 Just before serving, stir in the red currant jelly and wine.

❧ CUCUMBER, DILL, & SOUR CREAM SALAD ❧

INGREDIENTS

2 cucumbers, peeled
1 tsp salt
⅔ cup (150ml) sour cream
½ tsp sugar
black pepper
1 tbsp chopped fresh dill

THIS LIGHT AND REFRESHINGLY TANGY
SALAD COMES FROM AUSTRIA.

SERVES 6

1 Cut the cucumbers in half lengthwise. Scoop out the seeds and cut crosswise into thin slices. Spread the slices over a large dish and sprinkle with salt. Cover and leave at room temperature for 15 minutes.

2 Meanwhile, mix the sour cream, sugar, and pepper in a bowl.

3 Place the cucumber slices in a nylon sieve and press out the liquid. Pat dry on paper towels, then add to the sour cream mixture and turn gently to coat evenly.

4 Cover the cucumber salad and chill until required. Place in a serving dish and sprinkle with dill.

❧ CRANBERRY SAUCE ❧

INGREDIENTS

1 cup (250ml) water
½ cup (125g) sugar
4 tbsp red currant jelly
1lb (500g) cranberries
zest and juice of 1 orange
1 cup (125g) walnuts, chopped (optional)

ILLUSTRATED ON PAGE 161
CRANBERRIES ARE ALWAYS SERVED WITH
ROAST TURKEY IN NORTH AMERICA. ADD
CHOPPED NUTS FOR EXTRA TEXTURE.

SERVES 6

1 Gently heat the water, sugar, and red currant jelly in a saucepan, stirring occasionally, until the sugar has dissolved.

2 Add the cranberries and bring to a boil. Simmer uncovered for 15 minutes. Stir in the orange zest and juice, and the walnuts, if using. Let cool.

3 Place in a serving dish, cover, and chill until required.

A GERMAN CHRISTMAS DINNER

THIS HEARTY SPREAD IS REMINISCENT OF MEDIEVAL BANQUETS. A rich, warming soup is followed by roast goose stuffed with apples and nuts, a popular feast dish that is served with red cabbage and potato dumplings. The apples and nuts are highly symbolic: apples represent the tree of knowledge, while nuts stand for the mystery of life. A spectacular coiled strudel makes a splendid dessert, followed by stollen, the fruit-filled bread always baked for Christmas.

DESSERTS

THIS RICH ASSORTMENT OF DESSERTS will delight the eye as well as the palate. For a truly spectacular presentation, choose a dramatic coiled strudel filled with soft cheese and spices, or a Christmas pudding shaped like a fruity cannonball and crowned with a sprig of holly. For a lighter touch, try the Italian zuccotto, a delicious confection of cream, chocolate, and nuts encased in coffee-flavored ladyfingers, or a delicate vanilla-flavored cream, shaped in a ring mold and filled with colorful fruit and leaves. And for sheer self-indulgence, sherry trifle is hard to beat.

ENGLISH CHRISTMAS PUDDING

INGREDIENTS
12oz (375g) mixed dried fruit
7oz (200g) dried fruit salad (apples, apricots, mangoes etc.), chopped
½ cup (60g) sliced almonds
1 small carrot, coarsely grated
1 small cooking apple, coarsely grated
grated zest and juice of 1 lemon
1 tbsp molasses
⅓ cup (90ml) stout
1 cup (60g) fresh white bread crumbs
½ cup (60g) flour
1 tsp ground allspice
¼ cup (60g) dark brown sugar
4 tbsp (60g) butter, melted
1 egg

BY TRADITION THE CHRISTMAS PUDDING IS MADE ON "STIR UP SUNDAY" – THE FIRST SUNDAY BEFORE ADVENT. THE WHOLE FAMILY USED TO GATHER TOGETHER TO STIR THE PUDDING MIXTURE IN A CLOCKWISE DIRECTION AND MAKE A WISH. IT WAS BELIEVED THAT STIRRING COUNTERCLOCKWISE WOULD STIR UP TROUBLE. THIS PUDDING WILL KEEP FOR A YEAR IF WRAPPED SECURELY AND STORED IN A COOL PLACE.

SERVES 6

1 Lightly butter a 6in (15cm) round steamed pudding mold and place a round of nonstick baking parchment in the bottom of each half of the mold.

2 Mix the dried fruit, almonds, carrot, and apple in a large bowl. Stir in the lemon zest and juice, molasses, and stout until well blended. Cover with plastic wrap and leave in a cool place for a few hours, or overnight.

3 Add the bread crumbs, sifted flour, allspice, sugar, butter, and egg to the mixture. Mix together and stir well until thoroughly blended. Have ready a pan into which the pudding mold will fit comfortably.

4 Spoon the mixture into both halves of the mold so they are evenly filled. At this stage, you can insert silver coins or keepsakes, wrapped several times in waxed paper.

5 Place the two halves of the mold together, stand on the base, and fasten the clip firmly to keep the pudding secure. Carefully place the mold in the pan.

6 Half-fill the pan with boiling water, making sure the level of the water is not above the seam of the mold. Bring to a boil, cover, and simmer very gently for 5–6 hours. Add boiling water to the pan from time to time as required.

7 Remove from the pan and let the pudding cool in the mold. Carefully remove half the mold and leave until the pudding is completely cold. Turn out, wrap in plastic wrap or foil, and store in a cool place until required. Reheat before serving.

8 To reheat, remove the plastic wrap or foil, replace the Christmas pudding in the mold, and cook for 1 hour in a pan of boiling water, as described above. Place on a heated serving dish and serve with Cumberland Rum Butter (see below).

CUMBERLAND RUM BUTTER

INGREDIENTS
6 tbsp (90g) unsalted butter
½ cup (90g) light brown sugar
½ tsp freshly grated nutmeg
¼ cup (60ml) dark rum or brandy

CHRISTMAS PUDDING IS ALWAYS SERVED WITH A "HARD" SAUCE MADE OF CREAMED BUTTER, SUGAR, AND RUM OR BRANDY. THE COMBINATION OF THE COLD, HARD SAUCE WITH THE HOT, SOFT FRUIT PUDDING IS TOO ENTICING TO RESIST.

SERVES 6

1 Place the butter in a bowl or food processor fitted with a metal blade. Beat or process the butter until white and creamy.

2 Add the sugar and nutmeg and beat again until light and fluffy.

3 Add the rum or brandy one drop at a time, beating continuously until enough has been added to flavor the butter well. Take care not to overbeat, as the mixture might then curdle.

4 Pile the rum butter into a dish, cover, and leave in the refrigerator until firm. Serve a large spoonful with each serving of Christmas pudding.

TRADITIONAL SHERRY TRIFLE

INGREDIENTS

2 eggs, plus 2 yolks
2 tbsp (30g) superfine sugar
1 tbsp cornstarch
1¼ cups (300ml) milk
1 tsp vanilla extract
4oz (125g) sponge cake, thinly sliced
2 tbsp strawberry or raspberry jam
2 tbsp Madeira wine
1 tbsp brandy
1 pint (250g) strawberries or raspberries, halved
1¼ cups (300ml) heavy cream
8 blanched almonds and strawberry leaves, to decorate (optional)

TRIFLE WAS VERY POPULAR IN VICTORIAN ENGLAND, WHERE IT WAS ALSO KNOWN AS "TIPSY" CAKE. IT IS EXTREMELY RICH.

SERVES 8

1 Whisk the whole eggs, yolks, sugar, and cornstarch in a bowl until well blended.

2 Place the milk in a saucepan with the vanilla extract and bring to a boil. Pour the milk onto the egg mixture in the bowl, whisking well.

3 Rinse the pan, then strain the custard through a sieve back into the clean pan. Cook over low heat, whisking continuously, until it has thickened. Do not allow the custard to boil or it will curdle. Leave until cold.

4 Spread the sponge cake slices with the jam and place a layer, jam side down, in the bottom of a serving bowl. Mix together the Madeira wine and brandy and sprinkle over the cake slices. Repeat with the remaining cake slices and sprinkle over the remaining Madeira wine and brandy.

5 Cover the cake with two thirds of the strawberry or raspberry halves. Place the cream in a bowl and whip until it stands in peaks.

6 Fold two thirds of the cream into the cold custard until it is well blended and smooth. Spoon over the cake and fruit in the bowl and smooth the top.

7 Place the remaining whipped cream in a pastry bag fitted with a small star nozzle. Pipe the cream over the top of the custard and decorate with blanched almonds, the remaining strawberries or raspberries, and the leaves, if using. Chill until required.

ZUCCOTTO

INGREDIENTS

¾ cup (175g) coffee liqueur
20 ladyfingers
1¼ cups (300ml) heavy cream
¼ cup (30g) confectioners' sugar, sifted
½ cup (60g) pine nuts, toasted
2oz (60g) almonds, toasted and chopped
1 cup (150g) semisweet chocolate morsels
confectioners' sugar and cocoa, to decorate

THIS DESSERT ORIGINATED IN FLORENCE – IT IS SAID THAT THE SHAPE RESEMBLES THE CUPOLA OF THE CATHEDRAL. ZUCCOTTO MEANS "LITTLE PUMPKIN," AND THE PUMPKIN-SHAPED MOLDS ARE ONLY OBTAINABLE IN ITALY, BUT A ROUND GLASS BOWL MAKES A GOOD SUBSTITUTE.

SERVES 6

1 Line the bottom and sides of a zuccotto mold, or a 4 cup (1 liter) round-bottomed glass bowl with damp cheesecloth, leaving the excess overlapping the sides.

2 Place 4 tablespoons of the coffee liqueur in a shallow dish. Dip one ladyfinger at a time into the liqueur, then place lengthwise down the side of the mold, sugared side against the cheesecloth.

3 Repeat until the sides and bottom of the mold are completely lined, making sure there are no gaps and trimming the ladyfingers to fit tightly. Chill for 30 minutes. Reserve the remaining ladyfingers and any coffee liqueur remaining in the dish for the top of the mold.

4 Place the cream and confectioners' sugar in a bowl and whisk until very thick. Spoon one quarter of the cream into another bowl and mix in the nuts and ⅓ cup (60g) of the chocolate morsels until well blended.

5 Spread the cream and nut mixture carefully over the ladyfingers in an even layer, smoothing the surface. Chill.

6 Place the remaining chocolate morsels and coffee liqueur in a heatproof bowl over a pan of hot water. Stir occasionally until melted. Let cool.

7 Add the remaining cream to the melted chocolate mixture and fold in carefully until evenly blended. Fill the center of the mold with the chocolate cream and smooth the surface to make it level.

8 Cover the mold with the remaining ladyfingers and sprinkle with any remaining liqueur. Press down firmly. Bring the excess cheesecloth over the top of the mold, place a plate on the surface, and weight the top. Chill overnight.

9 Remove the weights and plate and fold back the cheesecloth. Invert the mold onto a serving plate and carefully remove the mold and the cheesecloth. Dust the surface thickly with confectioners' sugar, then dust alternate sections with cocoa, using a wedge-shaped template.

CELEBRATION STRUDEL

INGREDIENTS

6 tbsp (90g) unsalted butter, melted
13oz (400g) cream cheese
3 eggs, separated
¾ cup (175g) superfine sugar
1½ cups (175g) ground almonds
finely grated zest of 1 lemon
⅔ cup (125g) golden raisins
2 tsp ground cinnamon, plus extra for dusting
7oz (200g) phyllo pastry
confectioners' sugar, for dusting

ILLUSTRATED ON PAGE 167
STRUDEL CAN BE MADE IN MANY DIFFERENT SHAPES AND SIZES, BUT THIS LARGE COIL IS ONE OF THE MOST SPECTACULAR, AND IDEAL FOR A SPECIAL OCCASION.

SERVES 6

1 Preheat the oven to 350°F/180°C. Line a large baking sheet with foil and brush with melted butter.

2 Place the cream cheese, egg yolks, and half the sugar in a bowl. Mix together with a wooden spoon, then beat until smooth. Stir in the ground almonds, lemon zest, raisins, and cinnamon until evenly blended.

3 Whisk the egg whites in a clean bowl until stiff, then gradually add the remaining sugar, whisking well after each addition. Add to the cheese mixture and fold in gently until evenly mixed.

4 Brush one sheet of phyllo pastry with butter, keeping the remainder covered with a damp dish towel. Cover with a second sheet and brush again.

5 Spread 1 tablespoon of filling along the pastry 1in (2.5cm) in from the long edge. Roll the pastry over the filling into a long roll.

6 Arrange the roll in a spiral, starting at the center of the baking sheet. Repeat with the remaining phyllo pastry, butter, and filling to make another 7 rolls, adding them onto the spiral to form a tight coil shape.

7 Brush the coil with melted butter and bake in the oven for 35–40 minutes, until crisp and brown. Meanwhile, fold the remaining pastry in half and brush with melted butter. Cut out 6 holly leaves and bake for 2 minutes. Dust the coil with confectioners' sugar and cinnamon and serve warm or cold, decorated with the holly leaves.

FRUIT IN COGNAC

INGREDIENTS

1 cup (250g) granulated sugar
⅔ cup (300ml) water
3 peaches
3 pears
3 clementines
¼ cup (30g) cranberries
brandy or liqueur

THIS MAKES A SPLENDID CHRISTMAS PRESENT, PACKED IN A DECORATIVE JAR. USE A COLORFUL SELECTION OF FIRM, RIPE FRUIT.

SERVES 6

1 Place ½ cup (125g) of the sugar and the water in a saucepan. Heat gently, stirring occasionally, until the sugar has dissolved.

2 Pour boiling water over the peaches, leave for 1 minute, then peel, halve, pit, and cut into thin wedges. Peel, core, and slice the pears. Peel the clementines and cut off the white pith with a sharp knife. Cut the clementines into thin slices.

3 Add all the fruit to the syrup, bring to a boil, then cook over low heat for 8–10 minutes, or until the fruit is tender.

4 Transfer the fruit to a heatproof dish, using a slotted spoon, and add the remaining sugar to the syrup in the saucepan. Heat the syrup, stirring occasionally, until the sugar has dissolved.

5 Boil rapidly until the temperature reaches 230°F/110°C on a candy thermometer, or the thread stage is reached. Test by pressing a small amount of syrup between 2 teaspoons. When pulled apart, a thread should form.

6 When the syrup has cooled, pour into a measuring jug and add an equal quantity of brandy or liqueur. Pour over the fruit, cover, and chill until required. If giving the fruit as a present, spoon into a sterilized jar and fill to the top with the syrup and liqueur. Secure with a screwtop lid.

VANILLA CREAM MOLD

INGREDIENTS

1 envelope gelatin
3 tbsp cold water
2½ cups (600ml) heavy cream
2 tsp vanilla extract
2 tbsp (30g) superfine sugar
1lb (500g) assorted fruit, such as strawberries, raspberries, blueberries, and cherries
strawberry leaves, to decorate (optional)

ILLUSTRATED ON PAGE 173
THIS DELICATE CREAM FROM NORWAY IS IDEAL TO FOLLOW A SUBSTANTIAL MAIN DISH.

SERVES 6

1 Place the gelatin and water in a small bowl over a pan of hot water and stir until the gelatin has dissolved.

2 Whisk the cream, vanilla extract, and sugar until well blended. Add the dissolved gelatin and whisk until the mixture thickens. Pour the cream into a 3¾ cup (900ml) 7½ in (19cm) ring mold and leave in the refrigerator for 3–4 hours to set.

3 Dip the mold in warm water and invert onto a serving dish. Fill the center with mixed berries and arrange berries around the bottom of the mold. Decorate with strawberry leaves and serve with Berry Sauce (see opposite).

⇢ Berry Sauce ⇠

INGREDIENTS
1 pint (250g) raspberries
1 pint (250g) strawberries
½lb (250g) blueberries
⅔ cup (150ml) water
2 tsp arrowroot
4 tbsp cherry brandy

ILLUSTRATED ON PAGE 173
USE ANY ASSORTMENT OF FRESH SOFT
FRUIT IN SEASON.

SERVES 6

1 Place the berries and water in a saucepan and bring to a boil. Cover and simmer for 5 minutes. Pour into a food processor and blend until smooth, then strain, or press the fruit and juice through a sieve into a bowl.

2 Place the purée in a saucepan and bring to a boil. Blend the arrowroot with a little water until smooth. Add to the purée, stirring continuously until it comes back to a boil.

3 Simmer for 2 minutes, cool, and add the cherry brandy.

⇢ Blueberry Cheesecake ⇠

INGREDIENTS
1¼ cups (200g) all-purpose flour, plus extra
for dusting
10 tbsp (150g) unsalted butter, cut into pieces
¼ cup (60g) sugar
1 egg yolk
FILLING
6 tbsp (90g) sugar
1lb (500g) cream cheese
1¼ cups (300ml) sour cream
2 eggs
1 tsp vanilla extract
finely grated zest of 1 orange
¾lb (375g) blueberries
2 tbsp red currant jelly
confectioners' sugar, to dust

ILLUSTRATED ON PAGE 161
THE MELT-IN-THE-MOUTH TEXTURE OF THE
SWEET PASTRY MAKES THIS
CHEESECAKE IRRESISTIBLE.

SERVES 6

1 Sift the flour into a bowl, add the butter, and rub in finely with the fingertips until the mixture resembles bread crumbs. Stir in the sugar and egg yolk and mix together to form a firm dough, adding a little cold water if necessary.

2 Roll out the dough on a lightly floured surface, thin enough to line the bottom and sides of a 1¾in (4.5cm) deep, 8½in (21cm) loose-bottomed fluted flan pan. Trim edges. Prick the bottom and chill for 30 minutes. Preheat the oven to 375°F/190°C.

3 Line the pastry shell with nonstick baking parchment and a thin layer of dried beans, rice, or pie weights. Bake blind in the preheated oven for 15 minutes, until the pastry is firm, but not brown. Remove the pastry shell from the oven and cool on a wire rack, still in the pan. Remove the paper, and beans, rice, or pie weights, and reduce the heat to 300°F/150°C.

4 For the filling, place the sugar, cream cheese, cream, eggs, vanilla, and orange zest in a bowl and beat until smooth. Add one third of the blueberries to the mixture. Fold them in gently until evenly mixed.

5 Pour the mixture into the pastry shell and bake in the oven for 1 hour. Turn off the heat and allow the cheesecake to cool in the oven. When completely cool, release the pan and place the cheesecake onto a serving plate.

6 Melt the red currant jelly in a small saucepan and brush it over the top of the cheesecake. Arrange the remaining blueberries on top of the cheesecake and dust with confectioners' sugar to serve.

⇢ Pecan Pie ⇠

INGREDIENTS
1¼ cups (150g) all-purpose flour, plus extra
for kneading
¼ tsp salt
6 tbsp (90g) butter, cut into pieces
3 tbsp cold water
corn syrup, to brush
FILLING
4 eggs
1 cup (250ml) corn, golden, or maple syrup
6 tbsp (90g) unsalted butter, melted
1 tsp vanilla extract
2 cups (250g) pecans

ILLUSTRATED ON PAGE 161
THE RICH, NUTTY FLAVOR OF THIS PIE HAS
MADE IT A CLASSIC IN THE AMERICAN SOUTH.

SERVES 8–10

1 Sift the flour and salt into a bowl, add the butter, and rub in with the fingertips until it resembles bread crumbs. Stir in the water and mix to a firm dough with a fork.

2 Knead the dough on a lightly floured surface until smooth. Roll out and line the bottom and sides of a 9in (23cm) pie dish. Trim the edge, reroll the trimmings, and cut out 12 maple leaves with a leaf cutter. Brush the leaves with water and position around the rim of the pie. Chill for 15 minutes. Preheat the oven to 400°F/200°C.

3 Line the pie shell with baking parchment and bake blind (see above) for 10 minutes. Remove the paper and pie weights and cool. Reduce heat to 350°F/ 180°C.

4 To make the filling, whisk the eggs, then slowly add the syrup, whisking to blend well. Whisk in the butter and vanilla and stir in the pecans. Spoon into the pie shell.

5 Bake for 40–45 minutes until risen, golden brown, and set in the center. Let cool, then brush with corn syrup to serve.

NORWEGIAN CHRISTMAS BUFFET

In Norway, the emphasis is on fresh, healthy ingredients, even at Christmas. The country's clear mountain streams produce some of the best fish in the world – hence the popularity of gravlax, the famous cured salmon. Tender lamb, bred on the high pastures, is cooked French-style on special occasions, with garlic and herbs, and the favorite dessert, a molded cream, is filled with seasonal berries, the preferred choice being the rare Arctic cloudberry.

CAKES & COOKIES

CHRISTMAS IS THE TIME FOR CELEBRATION CAKES. Rich, dark fruit cakes, redolent of wine and spices, are made well in advance and left to mature. Later, they can be covered with marzipan and lavishly iced. Fruit breads such as panettone, gingerbread, and other spiced cakes are also traditional fare.

Macaroon cake, a fairy castle made of meringue, or festive pavlova, piled high with frosted fruit, would make a stunning centerpiece. Shaped cookies, decorated with icing and tied with ribbons, can be hung on the tree to delight the children, while the grown-ups feast on chocolate truffles.

➤ TWELFTH NIGHT CAKE ➤

INGREDIENTS

½ lb (250g) unsalted butter, softened, plus extra for greasing
1 cup (250g) dark brown sugar
⅔ cup (150ml) port
⅔ cup (150ml) brandy
1½ lb (750g) mixed dried fruit
4oz (125g) dried apricots, chopped
¼ cup (60g) mixed chopped peel
4oz (125g) glacé cherries, halved
1 tbsp grated orange zest
1 tbsp freshly squeezed orange juice
4 eggs
2 cups (250g) self-rising flour
1 tbsp ground mixed spice
¾ cup (90g) sliced almonds

DECORATION

3 tbsp apricot jam, boiled and sieved
1¾ lb (900g) white marzipan
confectioners' sugar, for dusting
2 quantities royal icing (see opposite)
red and green food coloring
2yd (2m) red or green ribbons

ILLUSTRATED ON PAGE 179

TWELFTH NIGHT CAKE USED TO BE SPECIALLY MADE TO MARK THE FEAST OF EPIPHANY. IT WAS ALWAYS A RICH FRUIT CAKE COVERED WITH ALMONDS OR ALMOND PASTE, BUT BY THE 19TH CENTURY THE CAKE HAD BECOME A MASTERPIECE OF DECORATION, WITH PIPING AND GILDING FAR BEYOND MOST COOKS' CAPABILITIES. TODAY, IT IS SIMPLY A CHRISTMAS CAKE, COVERED WITH MARZIPAN AND ICING.

MAKES A 9IN (23CM) CAKE

1 Place the butter, sugar, port, and brandy in a large pan and bring to a boil. Stir in the mixed fruit, apricots, mixed peel, and cherries until well blended. Return to a boil and simmer very gently for 15 minutes. Cool the mixture overnight.

2 Lightly grease a 9in (23cm) round cake pan. Line the bottom and sides with a double thickness of nonstick baking parchment. Secure a double thickness strip of brown paper around the outside of the pan, then set the pan on a baking sheet lined with three to four layers of brown paper. Preheat the oven to 300°F/160°C.

3 Beat the orange zest and juice with the eggs. Sift the flour and spice into a large bowl and stir in the almonds. Add the beaten eggs and the cooled mixed fruit to the flour, stir until well mixed, then beat for 1 minute.

4 Place the mixture in the prepared pan, smooth the top, and bake in the oven for 3–3¼ hours, or until a skewer inserted into the center of the cake comes out clean. Cool in the pan.

5 Turn out the cake, leaving the lining paper in place. Wrap the cake securely in foil and store in a cool place for up to 3–4 months until ready to decorate.

DECORATING THE CAKE

1 Place the cake in the center of a cake board and brush with the apricot jam. Knead three quarters of the marzipan into a round, reserving the remainder. Roll out the marzipan on a surface lightly dusted with confectioners' sugar to form a round 3in (7cm) larger than the top of the cake.

2 Place the marzipan over the cake and smooth the top and sides with your hands. Trim off the marzipan at the base of the cake. Leave in a warm place to dry overnight.

3 Knead the trimmings and reserved marzipan together. Color a tiny piece red. Cut the remainder in half and color one piece light green and the other dark green. Roll out the dark green marzipan until thin and cut out holly leaves, using a small cutter. Roll out the light green marzipan and cut out ivy leaves, using a small cutter. Mold tiny berries with the red marzipan.

4 Make the royal icing (see opposite). Using a narrow spatula, spread the top of the cake with a thin, even layer of icing. Hold a long narrow spatula at a slight angle and draw it across the cake toward you in a continuous movement to make a smooth surface. Leave for 3–4 hours to dry.

5 Repeat with a second layer of icing and leave to dry. Spread the remaining icing smoothly over the side of the cake. Using a small narrow spatula, press into the surface of the icing on the side and pull away gently to form peaks. Let dry overnight.

6 Arrange the holly leaves and berries on top of the cake and secure with a little icing. Fit the ribbon around the cake and the cake board and secure with a little icing. Leave in a cake pan in a warm dry place to set overnight. If uncut, the cake will keep in a tin for up to 1 year.

PANETTONE

THIS LIGHT, AIRY CAKE IS THE ITALIAN VERSION OF CHRISTMAS CAKE.

SERVES 6–8

INGREDIENTS

3½ cups (450g) unbleached all-purpose flour,
plus extra for dusting
1 tsp salt
3 tbsp (45g) superfine sugar
2 envelopes quick-rise dry yeast
¼ lb (125g) unsalted butter, melted
⅔ cup (150ml) milk
1 tsp vanilla extract
1 egg, plus 2 yolks
vegetable oil, for brushing
1 tbsp butter, plus extra for greasing
½ cup (125g) glacé fruits
½ cup (90g) golden raisins
2 tsp grated lemon zest
confectioners' sugar, for dusting

1 Sift the flour, salt, sugar, and yeast into a warm mixing bowl, or food processor fitted with a dough beater.

2 Add the melted butter to the milk. Beat in the vanilla, egg, and yolks. Mix into the flour to form a soft dough. Knead for 8–10 minutes, or 2–3 minutes in a food processor, until smooth and elastic. Brush with oil, cover with plastic wrap, and leave in a warm place for 1–2 hours, until doubled in size.

3 Meanwhile, lightly grease a 6in (15cm) round cake pan and line the bottom with nonstick baking parchment. Dust the inside with flour. Set the pan on a baking sheet and tie a piece of foil around the outside of the pan to stand 3in (7cm) above the rim.

4 Knead the dough for 1–2 minutes, until smooth, then roll out into a flat round. Mix together the glacé fruits, raisins, and lemon zest, scatter over the surface of the dough, and press in with the rolling pin.

5 Knead the dough until smooth. Gather into a ball and cut a cross in the top with scissors. Place in the cake pan, cover carefully with oiled plastic wrap, and leave in a warm place to rise until the center touches the wrap. Preheat the oven to 400°F/200°C.

6 Remove the plastic wrap, recut the cross, and place the tablespoon of butter in the center. Bake for 10 minutes, then lower the heat to 350°F/180°C and bake for 40–45 minutes, until a skewer inserted into the center comes out clean. Cool in the pan for 10 minutes, remove the foil, and ease the cake out of the pan. Cool on a wire rack. Dust with confectioners' sugar before serving.

WREATH CAKE

ILLUSTRATED ON PAGE 179

THIS SCANDINAVIAN CAKE MAKES A STUNNING CENTERPIECE FOR THE CHRISTMAS TABLE.

SERVES 10

INGREDIENTS

¾ cup (90g) almonds, chopped
½ cup (90g) golden raisins
½ cup (90g) dark raisins
½ cup (90g) glacé cherries, halved
¼ cup (60g) mixed chopped peel
2 tbsp sherry
1⅔ cups (175g) self-rising whole wheat flour
1 tsp ground cardamom
1 cup (175g) moist light brown sugar
12 tbsp (175g) unsalted butter, softened, plus
extra for greasing
3 eggs
3 tbsp apricot jam, boiled and sieved
1½ lb (750g) white marzipan
dark green food coloring
confectioners' sugar, for dusting
marzipan apples, pears, and oranges and holly
and ivy leaves (see page 178), to decorate
2 tbsp royal icing (see below)

1 Preheat the oven to 300°F/160C°. Grease a 9in (23cm) ring mold and place a circle of nonstick baking parchment on the bottom.

2 Mix together the almonds, golden raisins, dark raisins, cherries, mixed peel, and sherry.

3 Sift the flour and cardamom into a bowl and add the sugar, butter, and eggs. Mix well, then beat for 2–3 minutes, until smooth and glossy. Fold the fruit and nuts into the mixture until evenly distributed.

4 Place the mixture in the pan, smooth the surface, and cook in the oven for 1 hour– 1 hour 10 minutes, until the cake feels firm to the touch. Test by inserting a skewer into the center of the cake – it should come out clean. Allow the cake to cool in the pan, then invert onto a wire rack and remove the paper.

5 Brush the cake evenly with the apricot glaze. Color the marzipan leaf green and knead until evenly colored. Roll out on a surface dusted with confectioners' sugar to form a round 2in (5cm) larger than the cake. Cut a small circle out of the center, then place the marzipan over the center of the ring.

6 Ease the marzipan around the inside of the cake and smooth over the top and down the sides, trimming off the excess at the base. Place the cake on a cake board or plate, store in a box or tin with a lid, and leave in a warm dry place to set overnight.

7 Arrange the marzipan fruit and leaves evenly over the cake, bending the leaves to shape. Use a little royal icing to make them stick firmly.

ROYAL ICING

MAKES ENOUGH TO COVER A 6IN (15CM) CAKE

INGREDIENTS

2 egg whites
¼ tsp lemon juice
4 cups (500g) confectioners' sugar, sieved
1 tsp glycerin

1 Stir the egg whites and lemon juice in a bowl. Mix in enough confectioners' sugar to give the consistency of unwhipped cream.

2 Add the remaining sugar a little at a time, gently beating after each addition, until the icing is smooth and stands in soft peaks. Stir in the glycerin until well blended. Place in an airtight container, or cover the bowl with a damp dish towel until ready to use.
WARNING: RAW EGGS CAN TRANSMIT SALMONELLA. AVOID SERVING TO THE ELDERLY, YOUNG CHILDREN, AND PREGNANT WOMEN.

POLISH SPICED CAKE

INGREDIENTS
1 tbsp melted butter
1 tbsp fresh white bread crumbs
½lb (250g) butter
1 cup (250g) superfine sugar
¼ cup (60ml) water
3 eggs, separated
2 cups (250g) self-rising flour
1½ tsp ground mixed spice
2 tbsp (30g) chopped angelica
2 tbsp (30g) mixed chopped peel
¼ cup (60g) glacé cherries, chopped
½ cup (60g) walnuts, chopped
confectioners' sugar, for dusting
fresh holly, to decorate

THE MOST IMPORTANT HOLIDAY OF THE YEAR IN POLAND IS NEW YEAR'S EVE. SPICED CAKE IS ALWAYS SERVED, PREFERABLY WITH VODKA.

SERVES 6–8

1 Preheat the oven to 350°F/180°C. Brush an 8in (20cm), 6 cup (1.5 liter) fluted ring mold with melted butter and coat with bread crumbs.

2 Place the butter, sugar, and water in a saucepan and heat gently, stirring occasionally, until melted. Bring to a boil, boil for 3 minutes until syrupy, then allow to cool.

3 Place the egg whites in a clean bowl and whisk until they stand in stiff peaks.

4 Sift the flour and mixed spice into a bowl, add the angelica, mixed peel, cherries, and walnuts and mix well. Stir in the egg yolks.

5 Pour the cooled syrup into the flour mixture and beat with a wooden spoon to form a soft batter. Using a plastic spatula, gradually fold in the egg whites until the mixture is evenly blended.

6 Pour the mixture into the prepared mold and lightly smooth the surface. Bake in the preheated oven for 50–60 minutes, or until the cake springs back when pressed in the center. Turn out and cool on a wire rack. To serve, dust thickly with confectioners' sugar and decorate with a sprig of holly.

NORWEGIAN MACAROON CAKE

INGREDIENTS
1lb (500g) ground almonds
2 tbsp (15g) flour
2½ cups (500g) superfine sugar
1 tbsp finely grated lemon zest
1 tsp almond extract
3 egg whites, whisked
ICING
1 tsp orange-flower water
1 egg white
2 cups (250g) confectioners'
sugar, sifted
DECORATION
fresh fruit and bay leaves
confectioners' sugar,
for dusting

ILLUSTRATED BELOW
THIS CAKE IS A FAVORITE FOR BIRTHDAY, WEDDING, AND CHRISTMAS CELEBRATIONS. WARNING: RAW EGGS CAN TRANSMIT SALMONELLA. AVOID SERVING TO THE ELDERLY, YOUNG CHILDREN, AND PREGNANT WOMEN.

SERVES 20

1 Preheat the oven to 375°F/160°C. Line three or four baking sheets with nonstick baking parchment.

2 Mix together the ground almonds, flour, sugar, lemon zest, and almond extract in a bowl until evenly blended.

3 Gradually stir in enough egg white to form a soft but firm dough. Divide into manageable pieces and roll out each piece into a rope as thick as a finger.

4 To construct the cake, the "ropes" are cut into 12 graduated lengths, and formed into circles. Start by cutting a piece 4in (10cm) long. Form into a circle, pressing the ends together to join neatly, and place on a baking sheet.

5 Continue to cut lengths and make circles, increasing the length by 1in (2.5cm) each time, until there are 12 graduated circles in total, the largest measuring 15in (37.5cm) in circumference.

6 Bake the circles in batches for 20 minutes, until pale brown and firm. Let cool for 10 minutes, then slide onto a wire rack.

7 To make the icing, whisk the orange-flower water and egg white in a bowl. Gradually add the confectioners' sugar, beating well after each addition, until it is the consistency of thick cream. Continue to beat and add sugar until it stands in soft peaks.

8 Spoon the icing into a waxed paper pastry bag fitted with a No. 1 plain writing nozzle. Alternatively, snip the point off the end of the bag, half-fill with icing, and fold down the top.

9 Using a flat cake plate or a cake board, place the largest circle in the center. Spread with a little icing and place the next largest circle on top. Repeat until all the circles are stacked together. Pipe fine threads of icing in loops around each ring until evenly covered. Decorate the base and top with fresh fruit and bay leaves and dust with confectioners' sugar.

⟡ Pavlova ⟡

INGREDIENTS

5 egg whites
1¼ cups (290g) superfine sugar,
plus extra for frosting
½ tsp vanilla extract
1½ tsp vinegar
1½ tsp cornstarch
3oz (90g) white seedless grapes
3oz (90g) red seedless grapes
8 physalis, optional
3oz (90g) cherries
3oz (90g) strawberries
1¼ cups (300ml) heavy cream
⅔ cup (150ml) plain yogurt
½ cup (125g) mixed glacé fruits, chopped

ILLUSTRATED ON PAGE *178*
THE LIGHT CRISP MERINGUE WITH A
WHIPPED CREAM CENTER WAS NAMED IN
HONOR OF THE RUSSIAN PRIMA BALLERINA,
ANNA PAVLOVA. THIS FESTIVE VERSION IS
DECORATED WITH FROSTED FRUIT.

SERVES 6

1 Preheat the oven to 275°F/140°C. Line a baking sheet with nonstick baking parchment and draw a 9in (23cm) circle in the center. Turn the paper over.

2 Place 4 egg whites in a clean bowl. Beat by hand or with an electric beater until the whites are stiff. Gradually add the sugar, whisking well after each addition, until the meringue is thick.

3 Blend together the vanilla extract, vinegar, and cornstarch in a bowl and add to the meringue. Whisk until the meringue is thick and glossy and stands up in soft peaks.

4 Spoon the meringue into a large nylon pastry bag fitted with a large star nozzle. Pipe a ring of shells following the marked line. Fill in the center with a coil of meringue.

5 Pipe another ring of shells on top of the first ring and fill in the center with the remaining meringue. Alternatively, spread the remaining meringue inside the circle and smooth the top.

6 Bake in the oven for 1 hour, then turn off the heat and leave the pavlova for 2–3 hours to become cold, without opening the oven door. Store in an airtight container for up to 2 weeks, or until required.

7 Whisk the remaining egg white in a bowl. Place some superfine sugar in a bowl and line a wire rack with paper towels.

8 Cut the white and red grapes into small bunches, brush all over with egg white, then dip into the superfine sugar until coated evenly. Place on the paper-covered rack and leave in a warm place to dry. Frost the physalis, if using, the cherries, and the strawberries in the same way.

9 Whip the cream and yogurt in a bowl until just thickened. Add the glacé fruit and fold in gently. Spoon the fruit and cream into the center of the pavlova and decorate with the frosted fruit.

⟡ Mince Pies ⟡

INGREDIENTS

3 cups (375g) all-purpose flour, plus extra for
dusting
12 tbsp (175g) butter
2 tbsp (30g) sugar
1 egg yolk
12oz (375g) mincemeat
confectioners' sugar, to dust

THIS RECIPE DATES BACK TO MEDIEVAL TIMES.
MINCEMEAT WAS ORIGINALLY A MIXTURE
OF SHREDDED OR MINCED MEAT, DRIED FRUIT,
AND SPICES – HENCE THE NAME – AND THE
MINCE PIE WAS LIKE A MODERN MEAT PIE.
SINCE THEN THE RECIPE HAS BECOME
SWEETER, AND THE MEAT HAS DISAPPEARED.

MAKES 20

1 Preheat the oven to 400°F/200°C. Sift the flour into a bowl, add the butter, and rub in lightly with the fingers until the mixture resembles bread crumbs.

2 Using a fork, stir in the sugar, egg yolk, and enough cold water to form a soft dough. Knead gently on a lightly floured surface.

3 Roll out the pastry until thin and cut out 20 x 3in (7cm) rounds and 20 x 2in (5cm) rounds, using fluted cutters. Knead the trimmings together and reroll as necessary.

4 Dust 20 x 3in (7cm) tartlet pans with flour and line with the larger pastry circles. Prick the bottom of each with a fork and half-fill with mincemeat. Brush the edges of each smaller circle with water, invert, and press on top of each tart to seal the edges.

5 With the point of a knife, pierce a hole in the center of each tart lid to allow the steam to escape. Bake in the preheated oven for 15–20 minutes, until light brown. Cool on a wire rack before removing from the pans. Dust with confectioners' sugar before serving.

FESTIVE CAKES & COOKIES

THIS ENTICING COLLECTION OFFERS SOMETHING FOR EVERYONE, from a traditional English fruit cake, covered with royal icing, to the entrancing Scandinavian wreath cake, decorated with an intricate, interwoven pattern of marzipan fruit and leaves. An elegant pavlova, filled with frosted fruit and cream, strikes a lighter note. Other traditional offerings include rich chocolate truffles, shortbread, spiced cookies to hang on the tree, gingerbread men, and ginger pigs, tied with ribbons.

STOLLEN

ILLUSTRATED ON PAGE 167
THIS GERMAN FRUIT BREAD WILL KEEP FOR UP TO 1 MONTH, AND THE FLAVOR IMPROVES WITH KEEPING.

SERVES 12

INGREDIENTS

⅓ cup (60g) raisins
⅓ cup (60g) currants
⅓ cup (60g) candied citrus peel, chopped
¼ cup (60g) glacé cherries, halved
2 tbsp (30g) angelica, chopped
3 tbsp dark rum
3 cups (375g) unbleached all-purpose flour, plus extra for kneading
¼ tsp salt
2 envelopes quick-rise dry yeast
6 tbsp (90g) superfine sugar
1 tsp grated lemon zest
¼ tsp almond extract
½ cup (125ml) milk, warmed
2 eggs
¼ lb (125g) unsalted butter, softened
¼ cup (30g) sliced almonds
confectioners' sugar, for dusting

1 Mix the raisins, currants, peel, cherries, angelica, and rum in a bowl. Cover and leave for several hours, or overnight. Drain thoroughly, reserving the rum.

2 Sift the flour and salt into a warm bowl. Stir in the yeast, half the sugar, and the lemon zest.

3 Place the almond extract, warm milk, eggs, and reserved rum in a separate bowl. Whisk until blended evenly. Add this liquid to the flour with 6 tablespoons (90g) of the butter, cut into small pieces. Mix together with a wooden spoon and beat until smooth.

4 Turn the dough out onto a lightly floured surface and knead for about 10 minutes, until smooth and elastic. Alternatively, use a mixer or food processor. Melt the remaining butter. Place the dough in a clean bowl. Brush the bowl and dough with the butter, cover with plastic wrap, and leave for 30 minutes.

5 Knead the dough until smooth, return to the bowl, and cover. Place in a warm place until doubled in size, 1–2 hours.

6 Turn out the dough, punch it down to remove air bubbles, and knead into a round. Flatten out the dough to a thickness of ½in (1cm). Sprinkle the soaked fruit and the almonds over the surface, then press into the dough. Gather up and knead lightly to distribute the fruit. Roll out to form an oblong measuring 12 x 8in (30 x 20cm).

7 Brush with butter and sprinkle with the remaining sugar. Fold one end into the middle and press down. Bring the opposite side over the fold. Using floured hands, press down the ends and taper them slightly.

8 Line a jelly roll pan with nonstick baking parchment. Place the loaf on the pan and brush with melted butter. Cover loosely with a dish towel and leave until doubled in size, about 30 minutes. Preheat the oven to 375°F/190°C.

9 Bake in the oven for 30–40 minutes, until golden brown. Cool on a wire rack and dust with confectioners' sugar to serve. To keep, wrap securely in foil or plastic wrap.

GREEK HONEY CAKE

SPICED HONEY CAKE IS BEST MADE 2 MONTHS BEFORE CHRISTMAS TO ALLOW THE FLAVORS TO DEVELOP, AND TO ALLOW THE CAKE TO ABSORB THE SYRUP.

MAKES ONE 8IN (20CM) SQUARE CAKE

INGREDIENTS

1 cup (275g) clear honey
½ tsp ground cloves
½ tsp ground cinnamon
½ tsp ground nutmeg
6 tbsp (90g) butter, softened
½ cup (90g) dark brown sugar
3 eggs, separated
1 tsp baking soda
2 cups (250g) all-purpose flour
1 tsp baking powder
½ cup (90g) mixed dried fruit
½ cup (90g) walnuts, chopped
warm honey and walnut halves, to decorate

1 Line the bottom and sides of a 7in (18cm) deep square cake pan with nonstick baking parchment. Preheat the oven to 325°/160°C.

2 Heat the honey, cloves, cinnamon, and nutmeg in a saucepan, bring to a boil, then allow to cool.

3 Place the butter and sugar in a bowl and beat with a wooden spoon until light and fluffy. Add the egg yolks one at a time, beating well after each addition.

4 Add the honey mixture and baking soda and beat until smooth.

5 Sift in the flour and baking powder. Fold in gently using a spatula until all the flour has been incorporated.

6 Whisk the egg whites in a clean bowl until stiff. Fold gently into the mixture with the fruit and nuts until evenly blended, then pour into the prepared pan and smooth the top with a spatula or knife.

7 Bake in the oven for 1 hour–1 hour 10 minutes, until the cake is well risen and golden brown and the top springs back when pressed in the center.

8 Cool the cake in the pan, then turn out onto a wire rack and remove the lining paper. Wrap the cake in plastic wrap or foil and store for 1–2 days before eating as the flavor and texture improve with keeping. To serve, glaze the top with warm honey and decorate with halved walnuts.

Fougasse Christmas Bread

INGREDIENTS
*4 cups (500g) unbleached all-purpose flour, plus
extra for kneading
¼ tsp salt
2 envelopes quick-rise dry yeast
¼ cup (60g) light brown sugar
grated zest and juice of 1 orange
⅔ cup (150ml) olive oil, plus extra for oiling
2 eggs
an assortment of fresh, dried, and candied fruit,
such as apples, pears, figs, grapes, pomegranates,
dates, and raisins, nuts such as walnuts,
almonds, chestnuts, and hazelnuts, and
nougat and other candy*

ILLUSTRATED ON PAGE 153
THIS ENRICHED BREAD FORMS THE
CENTERPIECE OF THE "THIRTEEN DESSERTS"
OF PROVENCE AND SYMBOLIZES CHRIST.
THE TWELVE APOSTLES ARE REPRESENTED BY
LOCAL PRODUCE SUCH AS NUTS, NOUGAT,
AND FRESH, DRIED, AND CANDIED FRUIT.
THE DISPLAY IS LEFT ON THE TABLE AND
REPLENISHED AS NECESSARY UNTIL
TWELFTH NIGHT.

SERVES 12

1 Sift the flour and salt into a bowl, add the yeast, sugar, and orange zest, and mix together until evenly blended.

2 Measure the orange juice and add hot water to make 1½ cups (300ml). Pour into a bowl and beat with the oil and eggs. Add to the flour mixture and mix together with a wooden spoon to form a soft dough.

3 Turn out onto a lightly floured surface and knead for 10 minutes, until smooth and no longer sticky. Alternatively, use an electric mixer or food processor.

4 Place the dough in a clean, oiled bowl, cover with plastic wrap, and set in a warm place for at least 1 hour, until doubled in size.

5 Turn the dough out onto the floured surface and knead for 1–2 minutes, until smooth and elastic. Cut in half and roll out one piece into an 8in (20cm) round. Keep the remaining half covered.

6 Preheat the oven to 425°F/220°C. Transfer the dough round to an oiled baking sheet. Using a sharp knife, make 12 deep cuts, radiating out from the center. With lightly oiled hands, pull the dough gently to open up the cuts. Cover with oiled plastic wrap and let rise for 20–30 minutes. Repeat to shape the remaining dough.

7 Bake the bread for 20–25 minutes, until well risen and golden brown, covering loosely with foil to prevent overbrowning. Cool on a wire rack.

8 Place the bread on a tray or large platter surrounded by the 12 items representing the Apostles: fresh and dried fruit, raisins, nuts, and nougat.

Gingerbread House

INGREDIENTS
*6 tbsp (90ml) golden syrup
2 tbsp molasses
½ cup (90g) light brown sugar
6 tbsp (90g) butter
4 cups (500g) all-purpose flour, plus extra
for flouring
1 tbsp ground ginger
1 tbsp baking soda
2 egg yolks*
DECORATION
*1 quantity royal icing (see page 175)
assorted colored candy
confectioners' sugar, for dusting*

MANY GERMAN CUSTOMS ASSOCIATED WITH
CHRISTMAS DATE BACK TO THE MIDDLE AGES.
THE SPICED COOKIES AND CAKES ALWAYS
MADE AT THIS TIME ARE OFTEN ASSOCIATED
WITH SPECIFIC CITIES: GINGERBREAD
COMES FROM NUREMBERG.
SERVES 20

1 Cut out the templates for the house, using the guides on page 189. Preheat the oven to 375°F/190°C. Line 3–4 baking sheets with nonstick baking parchment. Place the syrup, molasses, sugar, and butter in a pan and heat gently, stirring occasionally, until melted.

2 Sift the flour, ginger, and baking soda into a bowl. Add the egg yolks and stir in the syrup mixture with a wooden spoon to form a soft dough. Knead on a lightly floured surface until smooth.

3 Cut off one third of the dough and wrap the remainder in plastic wrap. Roll out the piece of dough until thin on a baking sheet. Place the template for the side walls at one end and cut out neatly with a sharp knife. Repeat to cut another wall shape. Remove the trimmings, knead together, and reroll on another baking sheet.

4 Bake the cut-out wall shapes in the oven for 8–10 minutes, until the gingerbread is golden brown. Cool on the baking sheet. Repeat with the remaining dough to make the other walls, and the roof.

5 Make the royal icing following the recipe on page 175. Spoon some of the icing into a waxed paper pastry bag fitted with a No. 2 plain writing nozzle. Pipe lines, loops, and dots around the windows, doors, walls, and roof to decorate and leave flat to dry.

6 To assemble the house, pipe a line of icing on the side edges of the main walls and side walls. Stick them together on a 10in (25cm) cake board to form a box shape.

7 Pipe a line of icing following the pitch of the roof on both end pieces and along the top of the two roof pieces. Press gently into position. Use books or small boxes to support the underneath of each overhanging roof piece while the icing sets, about 15–20 minutes (see page 189).

8 Pipe the finishing touches to the roof and base of the house. Use icing to stick the colored candy along the seams and around the base of the house. Dust the cake board and house with confectioners' sugar.

New Year's Eve Fritters

INGREDIENTS
2½ cups (300g) all-purpose flour
¼ tsp salt
2 tbsp (30g) sugar
1 envelope quick-rise dry yeast
1 cup (200ml) milk, warmed
2 eggs
FILLING
⅓ cup (60g) currants
⅓ cup (60g) raisins
1oz (30g) crystallized orange peel, chopped
1 tbsp freshly grated lemon zest
vegetable oil, for deep frying
confectioners' sugar, for dusting

THESE DELICIOUS FRITTERS FROM HOLLAND ARE MADE WITH A YEAST DOUGH PACKED WITH FRUIT, CANDIED PEEL, AND LEMON ZEST. DROPPED INTO HOT OIL, THEY PUFF UP TO FORM CRISP, GOLDEN FRUIT DONUTS.

MAKES 20

1 Sift the flour and salt into a warm bowl, and stir in the sugar and yeast.

2 Add the milk and eggs and mix together with a wooden spoon to form a soft dough. Beat the dough until it is smooth and just holds its shape on the spoon.

3 Cover the bowl with plastic wrap and leave in a warm place for about 1 hour, until the dough has doubled in size.

4 Mix together the currants, raisins, peel, and lemon zest in a bowl. Add to the dough and stir until evenly distributed. Cover with plastic wrap.

5 Pour oil into a deep-fryer to a depth of about 3in (10cm). Heat the oil to 340°F/170°C, or until a cube of bread dropped into the oil browns in 30 seconds.

6 Using a tablespoon, scoop out one spoonful of dough and carefully drop into the oil. Fry 4 fritters at a time, turning them with a slotted spoon until golden brown. Drain on a wire rack covered with paper towels and repeat with the remaining dough.

7 Dust the fritters with confectioners' sugar and serve warm or cold.

St. Nicholas Spice Cookies

INGREDIENTS
2 cups (250g) self-rising flour
¼ tsp of each ground spice: cinnamon, nutmeg, anise, mace, cloves, cardamom, and ginger
⅔ cup (125g) light brown sugar
½ cup (60g) ground almonds
¼ lb (125g) unsalted butter, softened
1 egg, beaten
½ cup (60g) sliced almonds
2 tbsp (30g) currants
1 recipe royal icing (see page 175)
red, yellow, and green food coloring
24 x 6in (15cm) lengths of thin colored ribbon

ILLUSTRATED ON PAGE 178
IN HOLLAND THESE COOKIES ARE TRADITIONALLY SHAPED IN WOODEN MOLDS.

MAKES 24

1 Preheat the oven to 375°F/190°C. Line 3–4 baking sheets with nonstick baking parchment or waxed paper.

2 Sift the flour and spices into a bowl. Stir in the sugar, ground almonds, and the butter, cut into small pieces. Rub in with the fingers until the mixture resembles fine bread crumbs. Stir in just enough egg to bind the mixture together. Knead into a neat ball.

3 Roll out the dough until thin, and cut out shapes using a gingerbread man cutter or other cutters. Place the cookies on the baking sheets and decorate the gingerbread men with sliced almonds or currants. To make hanging decorations, make a hole at the top of each shape with a drinking straw. Bake for 10–15 minutes until golden brown. Cool on the baking sheet, then transfer to a wire rack.

4 Divide the royal icing into 3 portions and color them red, yellow, and green. Spoon each color into a waxed paper pastry cone, fold down the top, and snip off the point.

5 Outline some of the shapes with a line of icing, and fill in the shapes with lines and dots, varying the colors. Let dry in a cool place. Use colored ribbons to hang some of the cookies on the Christmas tree.

Marzipan Fruit

INGREDIENTS
8oz (250g) white marzipan
green, yellow, and orange food coloring
whole cloves, cut in half crosswise

DECORATE CAKES, OR THE CHRISTMAS TABLE, WITH THIS ASSORTMENT OF FRUIT.

MAKES 40

1 Divide the marzipan into 4 pieces. Color 2 pieces light and dark green; color the remainder yellow and orange.

2 Using pea-sized pieces, mold the light green, orange, and yellow marzipan into apple, orange, and pear shapes. Texture the oranges by rubbing gently on a fine grater. Insert a clove top into each fruit as a stalk, and the end as a calyx.

3 Using the dark green marzipan and a small leaf cutter, cut out holly, ivy, and grape leaves. Mark the veins by pressing a real leaf onto the marzipan leaf, then bend the leaves into shape.

4 Let dry in a warm place overnight. To decorate a cake, use a little icing to hold the shapes in position.

GINGER PIGS

INGREDIENTS

1⅓ cups (175g) self-rising flour,
plus extra for dusting
1 tsp ground ginger
1 tsp nutmeg
finely grated zest of 1 lemon
½ cup (90g) soft brown sugar
¼ lb(125g) unsalted butter
⅓ cup (60g) currants
1 egg, beaten
60 x 12in (30cm) lengths of thin colored ribbon

ILLUSTRATED ON PAGE 178
THESE CORNISH GINGER COOKIES ARE
BAKED IN MANY SHAPES – STARS, HEARTS, AND
GINGERBREAD MEN, AS WELL AS PIGS – TO
DISPLAY IN SHOPS AND MARKETS DURING
ADVENT, TIED WITH FESTIVE RIBBON.

MAKES 60

1 Sift the flour and spices into a bowl. Stir in the lemon zest and sugar. Rub in the butter finely with the fingers.

2 Add 3 tablespoons (45g) of the currants and the egg and mix to form a firm dough. Knead on a lightly floured surface until smooth. Wrap in plastic wrap and chill for 1 hour.

3 Line 2 baking trays with nonstick baking parchment or waxed paper and preheat the oven to 375°F/190°C.

4 Roll out the dough on a lightly floured surface until ¼in (5mm) thick. Using a pig-shaped cutter, or other cookie cutter, cut out about 60 shapes, kneading and rerolling the trimmings when necessary.

5 Arrange the shapes far apart on the baking sheets, press a currant in position for each eye, and bake in the oven for 10–15 minutes. Let cool on the sheet for 10 minutes, then transfer to a wire rack.

6 Tie each "pig" cookie around the neck with colored ribbon, and arrange on a serving plate, or tie onto the Christmas tree.

SCOTTISH SHORTBREAD

INGREDIENTS

1⅔ cups (175g) all-purpose flour,
plus extra for dusting
4 tbsp (60g) superfine sugar,
plus extra for sprinkling
½ cup (60g) cornstarch or ground rice
¼ lb(125g) unsalted butter, diced

ILLUSTRATED ON PAGE 179
SCOTTISH SHORTBREAD IS TRADITIONALLY
SHAPED IN WOODEN MOLDS AND CUT INTO
TRIANGLES CALLED "PETTICOAT TAILS."

MAKES 12

1 Preheat the oven to 325°F/160°C. Mix together 1 teaspoon each of flour and sugar and use to dust a 4in (10cm) shortbread mold, if available. If not, use 4in (10cm) cookie cutters. Line a baking sheet with waxed paper.

2 Sift the flour, cornstarch, and sugar into a mixing bowl. Rub in the butter finely with your fingers until the mixture begins to hold together. Knead into a firm dough.

3 Cut the dough into 12 pieces. Roll out one piece on a lightly floured surface to the size of the mold, if using. Place the dough in the mold and press to fit neatly. Using a narrow spatula, trim off the excess dough. Invert onto the baking sheet and tap firmly to release the shape. Repeat with the remaining dough, reflouring the mold each time.

4 If not using a mold, roll out the dough on a floured surface to a thickness of ¼in (5mm) and cut out 12 shapes with cookie cutters. Bake in the oven for 35–40 minutes until pale in color.

5 Sprinkle the top of the shortbread with a little sugar and let cool on the baking sheet.

CHOCOLATE TRUFFLES

INGREDIENTS

½ cup (125ml) heavy cream
2 tbsp dark rum, brandy, or sherry
½lb (250g) white, baker's semisweet, or
milk chocolate, melted and cooled
COATINGS
2 tsp cocoa
1 tsp confectioners' sugar
2oz (60g) white or baker's semisweet
chocolate, grated
2 tbsp chocolate sprinkles or chopped nuts

ILLUSTRATED ON PAGE 179
CHOCOLATE TRUFFLES ARE ALWAYS A FAVORITE
AT CHRISTMASTIME. PACK THEM INTO PRETTY
BOXES AS A GIFT, OR PILE THEM HIGH ON A
DECORATIVE PLATE.

MAKES 30

1 Place the cream in a pan, bring to a boil to sterilize, then cool until warm. Stir in the rum, brandy, or sherry when the mixture is lukewarm, then add it to the cool, melted chocolate, stirring until evenly blended.

2 Beat the mixture until light and fluffy, then chill for 2–3 hours until it is firm enough to divide into portions.

3 Using a teaspoon, scoop out balls of the mixture onto a tray lined with paper towels, keeping them about 1in (2cm) apart. Chill until firm, about 1 hour, then roll each portion of truffle mixture into a neat ball.

4 Sift the cocoa and confectioners' sugar together on a plate and roll some of the truffles in the mixture to coat evenly. Repeat, coating the remaining truffles in grated chocolate, chocolate sprinkles or nuts. Chill until set.

COUNTDOWN TO CHRISTMAS

TEN WEEKS AHEAD

✤ Read **Ultimate Christmas** for ideas
✤ Visit Christmas departments to see what is available
✤ Write out a gift list and decide what to make and what to buy
✤ Design and plan a gift-filled Advent calendar (see page 120)
✤ Design Christmas cards and gift wrap
✤ Gather odds and ends that will be useful for finishing touches,
such as leaves, seed pods, buttons, ribbons, sequins, beads, shells, and boxes

Shells
Collect seashells
on your summer
vacation, or buy
polished ones in
a shell shop

EIGHT WEEKS AHEAD

✤ Buy materials for cards, gifts, and Advent calendar
✤ Make Advent calendar (see page 120)
✤ Start making Christmas cards and gifts
✤ Make Christmas stockings (see page 118)
✤ Decide what type of tree to use (see pages 14–17)
✤ Plan theme for tree decorations and decide what to make and what to buy
✤ Make Greek Honey Cake (see page 180) and store wrapped in foil

SIX WEEKS AHEAD

✤ Begin gift shopping
✤ Start making tree decorations
✤ Check last mailing dates and buy stamps
✤ Plan your Christmas menu
✤ Add a few extra-special Christmas items to weekly shopping
✤ Make Twelfth Night Cake (see page 174), Wreath Cake (see page 175),
and Christmas Pudding (see page 168) and wrap in foil

Craft Dough Camel
(see pages 20–21)
Make craft dough tree
decorations six weeks
before Christmas

FOUR WEEKS AHEAD

✤ Print gift wrap (see pages 100–101)
✤ Make gift boxes to fit gifts (see page 102)
✤ Start using Advent calendar and let children write to Santa
✤ Plan theme for dining table and make festive table decorations,
such as crackers (see pages 142–43) and painted glassware (see pages 126–27)
✤ Make decorations using dried and artificial ingredients, such as wreaths
(see pages 50–55), door swags (see pages 56–57), and garlands (see pages 60–63)
✤ Plan lighting, such as lanterns (see page 86–87) or a twig chandelier (see page 80)
✤ Order special food as necessary, such as fresh turkey, goose, or fish

TWO WEEKS AHEAD

❧ *Get table linen laundered and decorate if desired (see pages 130–31)*
❧ *Buy a fresh tree and keep it in water in a cool place;*
bring it indoors as late as possible
❧ *Test tree lights and replace broken bulbs*
❧ *Look for supplies of holly and evergreens*
❧ *Stock up on candles*
❧ *Shop for nonperishable food*
❧ *Make dishes that can be frozen, such as stuffings (see pages 158–59),*
soups (see pages 148–49), and mince pies (see page 177)
❧ *Ice Twelfth Night Cake (see page 174)*
❧ *Make Panettone (see page 175) and store in foil*
❧ *Make Pavlova shell (see page 177) and store in an airtight container*

Embroidered napkins
(see page 131)
Use gold thread to
embroider a festive
motif on table napkins

ONE WEEK AHEAD

❧ *Decorate the tree*
❧ *Wrap and decorate gifts*
❧ *Make decorations using evergreens, such as*
a kissing bough (see pages 68–71)
❧ *Make gingerbread angels for the tree (see page 40)*
❧ *Decorate the house with store-bought and homemade decorations*
❧ *Make Cranberry Sauce (see page 165)*
❧ *Make Truffles (see page 183) and refrigerate*
❧ *Make Cumberland Rum Butter (see page 168)*
❧ *Make Gingerbread House pieces (see page 181) and store in a cake box*
❧ *Make cookies and shortbread (see pages 182–83), and store in an airtight container*

Gift boxes
(see page 102)
Start to wrap gifts one
week before Christmas

THREE OR FOUR DAYS AHEAD

❧ *Arrange flowers (see page 66–67)*
❧ *Make a fresh garland (see page 60–63)*
❧ *Shop for last-minute food items*
❧ *Make or buy lots of ice for festive drinks*
❧ *Boil ham and refrigerate (see page 156)*

CHRISTMAS EVE

❧ *Make a fruit and flower display (see page 72)*
❧ *Prepare as much of the festive meal as possible*
❧ *Defrost frozen food, allowing 24 hours for large turkeys or geese*
❧ *Set the table if possible*
❧ *Put champagne on ice*
❧ *Hang stockings*

Fresh holly
Make fresh decorations as
close to the day as possible

TEMPLATES

Use the templates on the following pages for specific projects,
or simply to help design festive gift tags, cards, block prints,
and tree decorations. The grid will help you to enlarge or
reduce the designs proportionally.

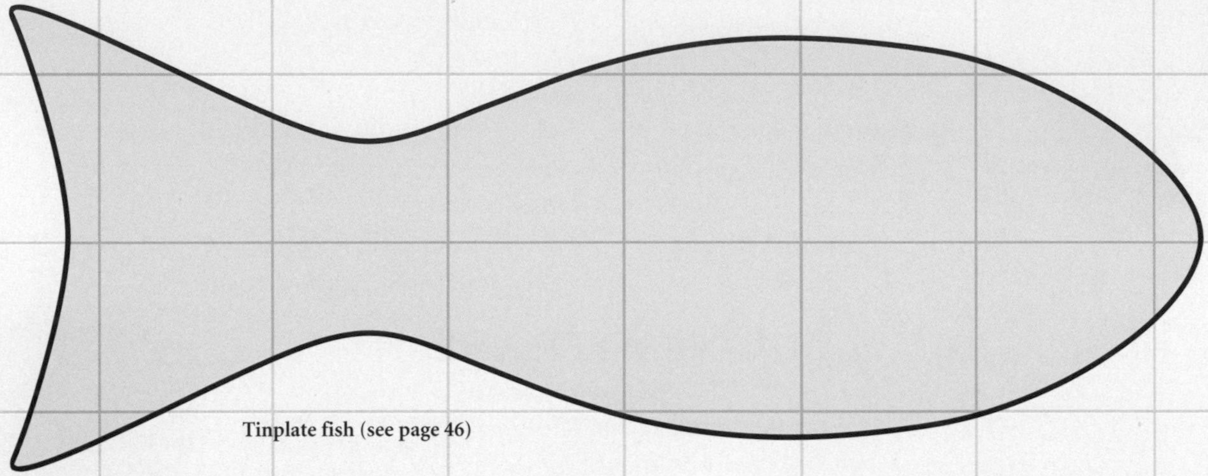

Tinplate fish (see page 46)

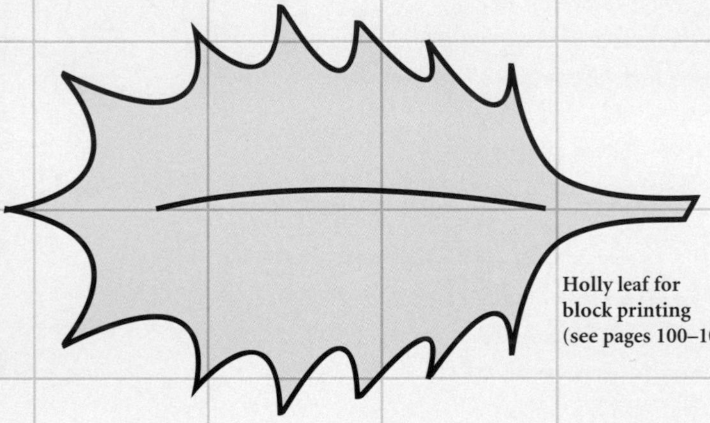

**Holly leaf for
block printing**
(see pages 100–101)

Heart for gift tags
(see pages 110–11)

Numbers for Advent calendar (see pages 120–21)

0 1 2 3 4

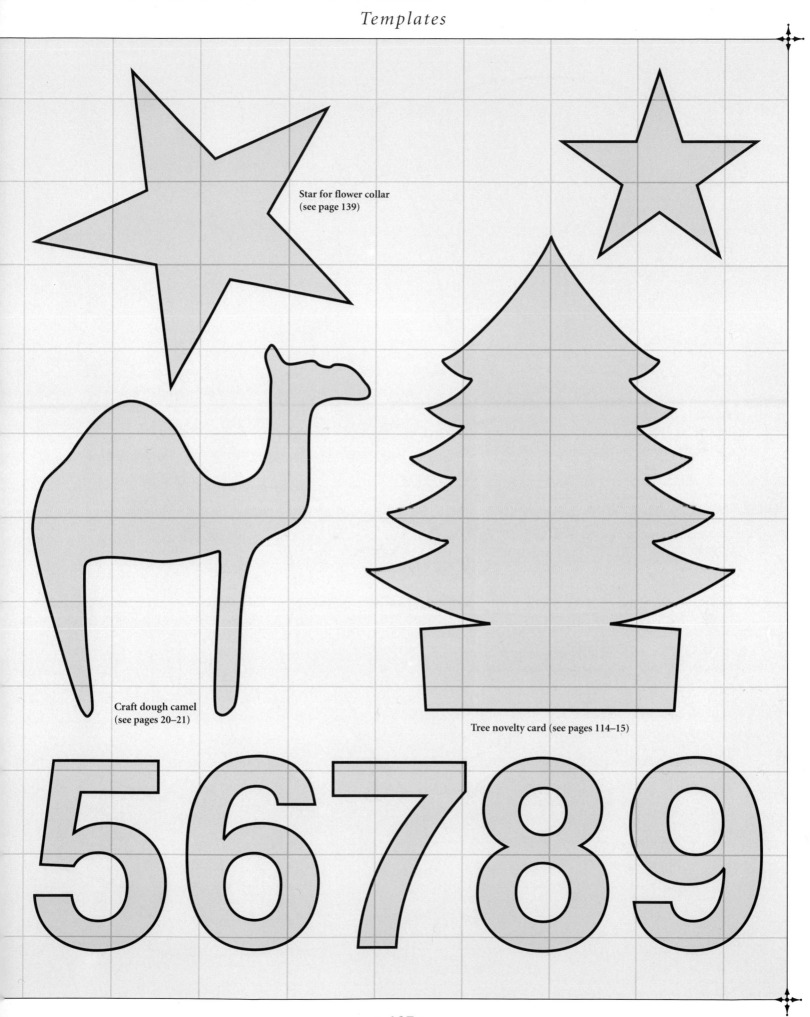

Star for flower collar
(see page 139)

Craft dough camel
(see pages 20–21)

Tree novelty card (see pages 114–15)

Sheep novelty card (see pages 114–15)

Gingerbread angel (see page 42)

Gingerbread angel (see page 42)

GINGERBREAD HOUSE (See page 181)

Assemble the house on a cake board, using royal icing to stick the pieces together. First form wall pieces B and C into a box shape. Pipe icing along the roof ridges of end pieces C and along the top of the roof pieces A, and press into position. Support roof overhang until dry, about 15 minutes.

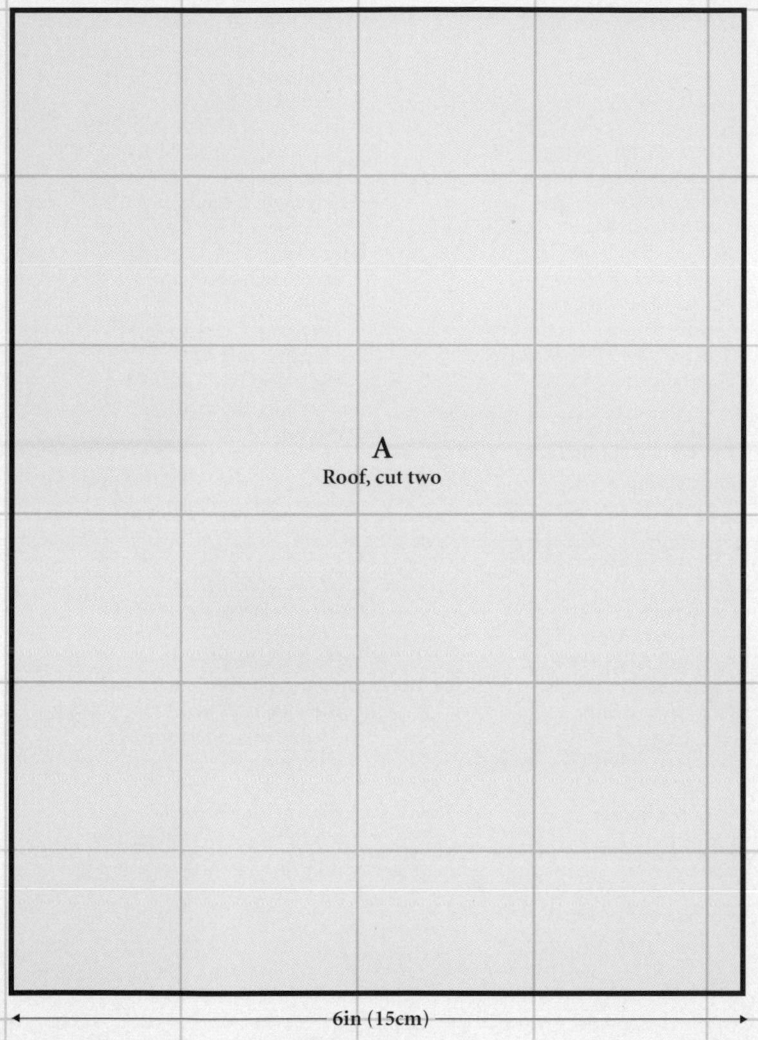

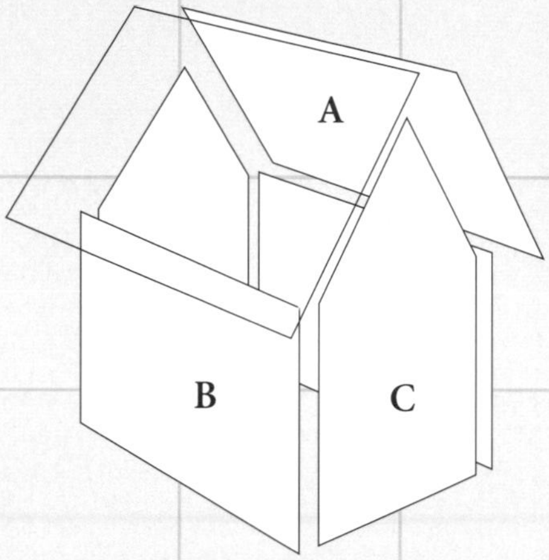

Assembled gingerbread house

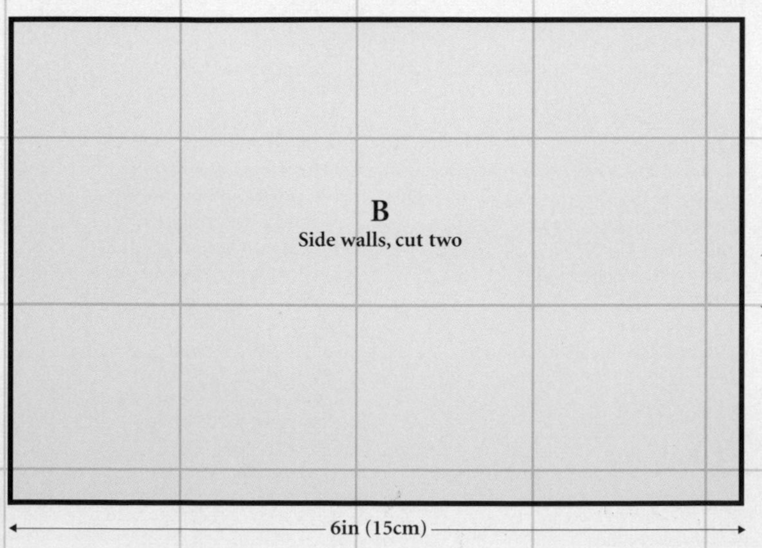

A
Roof, cut two

8in (20cm)

6in (15cm)

B
Side walls, cut two

4in (10cm)

6in (15cm)

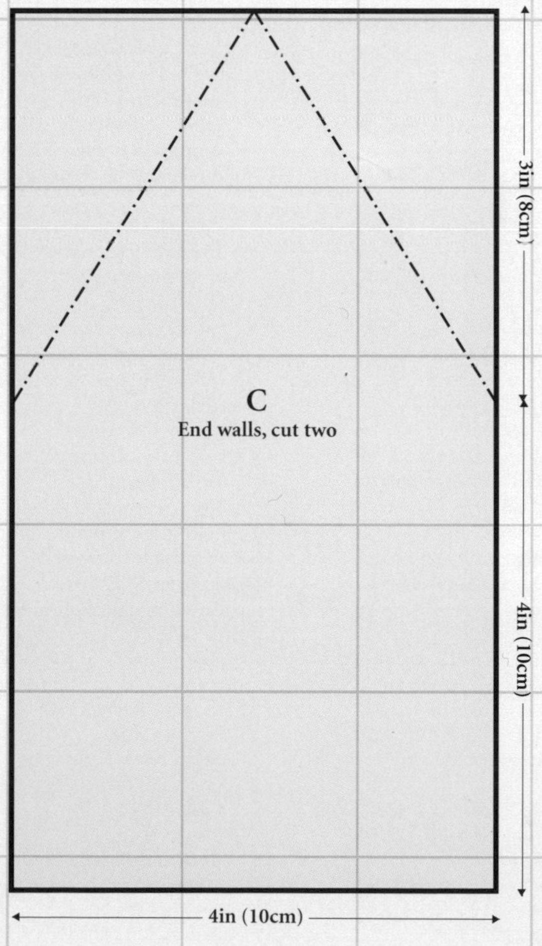

C
End walls, cut two

3in (8cm)

4in (10cm)

4in (10cm)

*I*NDEX

ACKNOWLEDGMENTS

AUTHOR'S ACKNOWLEDGMENTS

I would like to thank everyone at Dorling Kindersley who worked so hard on this project: Susannah, Carole, Toni, and Tracey for their support and ideas and for keeping us all motivated and on schedule. Thanks, too, to Dave King for being such a patient and creative photographer as well as providing delicious eclectic lunches, upbeat music, and good company at all times. Kate, the Art Editor, was wonderfully calm, professional, and careful during the photo shoots, working incredibly hard to make the book look spectacular, and Annabel has been the perfect editor. As well as adding a great deal of style to the words, she gently but efficiently guided the whole project along and managed to make it feel easy – which was no mean feat. Thanks should go to Kylie, Alexa, and everyone else in the team.

PUBLISHER'S ACKNOWLEDGMENTS

Dorling Kindersley would like to thank Lucy Parissi and Emy Manby for design assistance; Linda Sonntag and Kirsten MacKinnon for editorial assistance; Clifton Nurseries for the blue spruce on pages 14 and 18, the holly tree on pages 14 and 28, the bay tree on pages 14 and 44, and the Versailles Box on page 14; Texas Home Care for the mantelpiece on pages 88-95, 116-19.

Food Stylist: Janice Murfitt
Props Stylist for Food: Helen Trent
Photography by Dave King, except: Martin Brigdale 144–48, 152–54, 158, 159 (t), 160–61, 165–67, 169, 172–73, 176–79, 182–83.
Index: Kate Chapman

Thanks to:
Clifton Nurseries Ltd., Clifton Villas, Little Venice, London W9. Tel: 0171 289 6851
The Flower Barn, Barnham, Chichester, West Sussex. Tel: 01243 553490
Spriggs Florist, Golden Square, Petworth, West Sussex. Tel: 01798 343372